BRIDGING GENERA[TIONAL] GAPS:

A PSYCHOLOGICAL PERSPECTIVE ON THE HADDOCK FAMILY

Billy D Haddock

Assisted by

Maredia Haddock Cunningham

DEDICATION

This book is dedicated to all my ancestors: past, present and future with prayers for continued spiritual growth. It is specifically dedicated to my daughter, Kristina, for whom I have eternal love.

I hope you find the words contained herein useful, enlightening and uplifting.

Billy D. Haddock, 2017

AVENT '91

1

---

[1] Wolf is the pathfinder, the forerunner of new ideas who returns to the clan to teach and share medicine. Wolf takes one make for life and is loyal like Dog. If you were to keep company with Wolves, you would find an enormous sense of family within the pack, as well as a strong individualistic urge. These qualities make Wolf very much like the human race. As humans, we also have an ability to be a part of society and yet still embody our individual dreams and ideas. – J. Sams

Contents

PREFACE

Carl Jung, a Swiss psychoanalyst, wisely said that we cannot move into the future with any certainty unless we are grounded in the past and in the Earth where we live. Many Native Americans knew that major decisions should be weighed carefully and made with the intent that the seventh generation down the genealogical line would be favorably affected. It seems to me that many wise and thoughtful people in this world recognize the influence of the past on present and future experiences.

This book represents an attempt to bridge past, present, and future so that we may learn to honor: the past as our teacher, the present as our own creation (and responsibility), and the future as our inspiration. This book also represents a search for pieces to the puzzle of my own identity and is offered for present and future generations to use in their search. Finally, my search in collecting this information has been a healing experience. I am hopeful it will stimulate others in searching for areas in their lives where relationships need healing.

Integrated in the family history, you will find elements of my personal interests in life: history, psychology, spirituality, animals, and Native Americans. This information is provided as food for thought and to expand our view of how "who we are" may be influenced by so many other complicated factors. Paradoxically, the answer to the question, **"who am I?"** can be simply stated as, "a living expression of God's creative spirit." This can be a simple truth if we aim at living on a higher level, a level that honors God's spirit in all of life.

As one might imagine, this work represents a departure from a purely historical quest. It looks beyond the simple facts of family history by including legend and psychological conjecture. It has been said that if one wants to know an entire people then sing their love songs and recite their prayers. These tell the whole story. In this family history, there is an attempt to tell the whole story, which included revealing some bits of information that may be painful to know. However, I believe we must overcome the tendency to ignore the negatives of the past and should embrace the painful truth about our family if we are to move forward positively into the future.

Therefore, this is a family tree that I hope will flower in your understanding as you take the things discussed in the following pages to heart and apply them to your daily living.

This work is organized into several sections which relate to the history of the Haddock family. Beginning in the British Isles in the first part, we move to the New England area to explore our best idea of how the Haddocks migrated to the United States. Part III begins the documented history of the Haddocks and traces them to the Texas area in the remaining sections. Additional information to support the narrative is included in the various Appendices.

I hope you enjoy this journey through the family history and better understand your own journey as you complete reading this work.

\- Billy Dan Haddock
  October, 1991

Preface to the 2nd Edition

Since October 1991, my sisters and I have continued to research family history, mostly during the winter months when weather in Texas hindered outside activities. With retirement came the luxury of having more time to spend in research and this second edition reflects new connections that weren't available in the earlier edition. For example, we now have identified all direct descendants going back to the earliest recorded history available in the British Isles. Since many English Haddocks were ship captains, additional research on the British navy has also been included in this edition.

Organization of the material is essentially the same. The wolf image is symbolic of pathfinder and teacher. We have both in our family history. Linkages to our British ancestors are made to document who came to America and when. Also, maiden names of women who married a Haddock ancestor is written in **ALL CAPS** to help maintain their family names. In addition, a few stories of ancestors who lived more daring lives have been included to add interest. These can be seen when a **spotlight** and/or **detour** is mentioned in the body of the book. Some of the original appendices and family tree charts have been preserved (in the back section) while additional appendices were added. For example, the original appendices that revealed a brief history of some families who married Haddock men have been preserved from the first edition (also in the back section). Sources of data are referenced and updated, as needed. Many sources came from ancestry.com and one must have a subscription to access these, so they are omitted.

In the earlier edition there may have been a few errors. Hopefully, these have been corrected. As with most research, it is an ongoing project. Areas for further investigation are mentioned throughout the text.

Enjoy!

- Billy D. Haddock 2017

ACKNOWLEDGMENTS

My sisters, Maredia Haddock Cunningham and Odessa Haddock Jackman contributed much time and effort in gathering the information for this family history. Maredia has continued consistently through the years and contributed immeasurable work on finding the graves of our ancestors. My brothers and many other relatives have also contributed to this piece of work. The original work of Thomas C. Haydock, Jr. of Cincinnati, Ohio and Florida maintained an ongoing interest in the Haddock family history and helped clarify some questions about the early family history. His work still serves as a useful reference when trying to connect relatives who may have undergone a name change and/or spelling change. All relatives who have done their own genealogy work and published it must be acknowledged. I hope your work has adequately been recognized in the bibliography. Finally, it should be noted that I have borrowed heavily from the previous work of other relatives. The words you find printed inside reflects a partially complete puzzle of which many pieces were simply put together. For the serious family researcher, I encourage you to continue this work. Other puzzle pieces may be found and added as they become available.

Billy D. Haddock

2017

PART I

Origins: Early Haddocks

Recorded history shows the American Haddocks originating from the British Isles. Haddock is considered an uncommon surname. Approximately 15,148 people bear this name in the entire world. (http://forebears.io/surnames/haddock, 2012)

Origins of name: ADDA

The name Haddock most likely came from the Anglo-Saxon ADDA, which in turn originated from EAD-WIG, meaning "fortunate in war". William, a popular name for sons of the Haddock family, also had a German derivation meaning "helmet of resolution". In everyday language, we might simply call this "stubborn".

When it comes to names, the first thing is not to be fussy. Though you may consider only one spelling of your name correct, chances are that several spellings were current in the 16th - 17th century. Even of the simplest - such as "Evans," "Johnson," and "Jones. Many names comprising but one long syllable was - and still are - spelled in many ways; for instance, "Kean," "Keane," "Keen, "Keene"; "Read," "Reade," "Reed," "Reede," "Reid," "Ried," and "Riede." When the long syllable ends with a sound that can be represented by either of two consonants, the number of possibilities grows; for instance, "Pearce," Pearse,"" Peerce," "Peerse," "Peirce," "Peirce," "Peirse," "Pierce," and "Pierse."

> The twenty-first century is like the seventeenth in having these variations but unlike it in worrying about them. As they were illiterate, most people of the seventeenth century *couldn't* worry about them, and the few who could probably didn't, for the notion that one spelling was correct and all others wrong didn't yet exist. Within limits, all spellings were acceptable. What mattered was sound. This is the view which twenty-first-century readers should take of seventeenth-century spelling.

Most variations found on the Haddocks are: Haydock, Hadduck, Shaddock, Headach, Haddox, Hattox, or Haddix. Many of the variations are due to auditory translations. The name was written and spelled out like it sounded, rather than how it was formerly spelled. This may have been, in part, due to illiteracy. Even in the United States, one can see how the Haddock name may have been changed. At least in one instance, the name was changed deliberately, to avoid prosecution from the law.

Therefore, take care to include variant spellings of the family names and you may find some good stories.

Origins of places

Milton Place

Printed sources record John, who died in 1327, as the first known Haddock but there was also William Haddock living in 1309. To meet him, we must journey to an ordinary medieval manor. This manor of Milton has been identified by three different names: Milton Place, Milton Road and Milton Street. Even now, there is a conservation district in England named Milton Place that has conserved the history of the area.

Here is a brief history of its origins:

798AD - Archbishop of Canterbury acquired a large landholding in North fleet, a small community established next to Thames River centered on a landing place ("hithe").

1086 - Reference to the Manors of Gravesham and Meletune (Milton).

1189 – Hospital founded on the future site of Milton Chantry.

1300 - Gravesend had grown into a small market town via its trade on the river and easy supply of supplies from neighboring agricultural land.

1322 - Milton Chantry founded by Aymer de Valence. The chapel still stands at Gravesend Riverside Conservation Area within the New Tavern Fort. It was a religious institution that owned Milton Place, originally, and is now listed as a Conservation Area Character Appraisal 2009 with considerable land in the area, on the outskirts of the fledgling town.

The town grew under various lordships including the crown, nobility and the Cistercian Abbey of the St Mary Graces in London.

1380 - French and Spanish warships attacked Gravesend. Most of the town was destroyed. In recompense Richard II granted the people of Gravesend sole rights to ferry passengers to London giving rise to Gravesend's growth as a maritime center and trading port.

Gravesend Watermen operated open barges, the Long Ferry, and transported passengers to and from the Pool of London. Larger, ocean-going vessels continued out along the estuary to the international destinations beyond.

River related occupations, including, ferrying, victualling, rope and sail making and boat building and repairing, occupied most the town's inhabitants. (http://docs.gravesham.gov.uk/WebDocs/Environment%20and%20Planning/Conservation_Areas/Milton_Place_Appraisal.pdf)

On a modern map of England, Milton Place is located near the ancient town of Gravesend.

William Haddock was one of nine free tenants on the manor who rented four acres of land from his lord. This was known as Heyrones land-tenement. William Haddock paid his rent in the form of attendance at the manor court and two shillings at Michaelmas (Christmas). Haddock was not listed as one of the tenants before 1309. Unfortunately, we can gather nothing of William Haddock's character or personal life from this extent, except that unlike the miserable serfs, William was free to live where he pleased and exempt from the drudgery of boon work. (Warwicker, 1973).

Chelmsford

Most of the records show Haddocks living in and around one area of England, Chelmsford, for centuries. Chelmsford is the principal settlement of the City of Chelmsford and the county town of Essex, in the East of England.

In 1199, following the commissioning of a bridge over the River Can by Maurice, Bishop of London, William of Sainte-Mère-Eglise was granted a Royal Charter for Chelmsford to hold a market, marking the origin of the modern town. An under-cover market, operating Tuesday to Saturday, is still an important part of the city center over 800 years later. The city's name is derived from *Ceolmaer's ford* which was close to the site of the present High Street stone bridge. In the Domesday Book of 1086 the town was called *Celmeresfort* and by 1189 it had changed to *Chelmsford*. Its position on the Londinium – Camulodonum Roman road ensured the early prosperity of Chelmsford; in the first decade of the 12th century its population had grown to several hundred, which was large for its time.

Before 1199, there were settlements nearby from ancient times. A Neolithic and a late Bronze Age settlement have been found in the Springfield suburb, and the town was occupied by the Romans. A Roman fort was built in AD 60, and a civilian town grew up around it. (From Wikipedia, the free encyclopedia)

It was in this area that the recorded history of the Haddocks as a family is found. While fuzzy about the details, we have records of a Richard Haddock living in this part of England from 1430 to 1483. Then

John Haddock, a son, from 1453 to 1483. It's interesting to see that all four (parents & wives) are listed as dying in the same year, so the records may be approximate. Another explanation of death may relate to the 'sweating sickness', that first appeared in England that year. Also, there happened such a flood in Gloucestershire, England that all the country was overflowed by the River Severn; several persons were drowned in their beds. In 1483, the River Severn in England overflowed during ten days, and carried away men, women, and children, in their beds, and covered the tops of many hills; the waters settled upon the lands, and were called "the Great Waters" for 100 years after. This event occurred during the first year of King Richard III's reign. [Another account places this event in 1485] In 1485 in England, for a long time there were continual rains and great moisture, swelled rivers. Especially the River Severn, which was so high for 14 days that it overflowed the whole country. It drowned many people in their beds, overturned houses, carried about children swimming in their cradles, drowned beasts grazing on the hills. However, the River Severn was west of London, where the Haddocks lived was east of London. So, I would rule out this alternative in favor of the 'sweating sickness' or just poor records.

I ran across a book that has documented the early Haddocks in Leigh through effigies found in the area. Somewhat like funeral-type shrines, effigies made of brass or other materials were popular in medieval times. This book gave more specific information regarding the families, including the death date of Richard Haddock and the direct link to his son, John. (The reliquary and illustrated archaeologist, 1895).

xt) - View all

The brass is unique (at least as far as Essex is concerned) in respect of the facts that it represents four principal effigies (a father and mother, with their son and daughter-in-law) all placed in a row, together with no fewer than twenty-one children (in two families), one of which unquestionably represents John Haddock, the son, who is thus represented by two effigies on one brass.

The two principal male effigies (both 1 ft. 4 ins. in height) are very closely similar. Both wear long fur-trimmed gowns, extending to the ankles, slit up a short way at the bottom in front, girt by a belt at the waist, and having loose sleeves gathered at the wrists. The shoes are long and pointed, and of one piece with the hose. The head is bare and the hair is cut in a manner which suggests the wearing of a wig.

The two principal female effigies (both 1 ft. 3 ins. in height) also very closely resemble one another. They wear long fur-trimmed gowns, falling in folds about the feet, slightly open at the neck, girt below the breasts, and having large loose sleeves, which fit tightly at the wrists. Both wear the "horned" head-dress usual at the period, consisting of a kerchief thrown over a wired erection, which was lowest in the middle. The children all wear costumes similar in general to those of their parents.

The Latin inscription below the chief figures may be thus translated :—" Here lie Richard Haddock and Christina and Margaret his wives ; also John Haddock, son of the said Richard and Christina, and Alice, wife of the said John ; which said Richard died the 11th day of November, in the year of our Lord, 1453 ; on whose souls may God have mercy." The supplication at the end has been intentionally obliterated, probably by a descendant in post-Reformation times, in order to save it from destruction by bigoted Puritans.

The Haddocks were closely associated with Leigh from the beginning of the fourteenth century till quite recent days. In the seventeenth and eighteenth centuries the family contributed many distinguished members to the naval service of the country, including two admirals and several captains.

Of a priest in academic costume, of the end of the fifteenth century (probably about 1480), we have a good, though rather small,

I would encourage the interested researcher to obtain the actual source for more information. I am providing 3 screen shots from the book that reference the Haddocks.

a whole effigy (originally about 21 inches in height), of which the lower half has disappeared, as has the inscription and also the companion (female) effigy which, doubtless, once accompanied it. It has been detached from its original slab and re-set in the cement which fills a larger matrix in another slab, now lying in the centre of the nave. The man is represented clean-shaven and his hair is close-cropped in a manner which suggests the wearing of a wig. His long gown (which extended, doubtless, to the level of his ankles) has extremely loose baggy sleeves, gathered at the wrists, and is not confined at the waist by a belt, as was usual. The cuffs and collar are narrowly fur-trimmed, as was, doubtless, the bottom edge of the garment. Except in the absence of the belt, the figure almost exactly resembles those of Richard Haddock and John Haddock (1453), at Leigh, near Southend. Another figure of somewhat the same type is that to William Lucas (about 1460) at Wenden Lofts. It is now quite impossible to name the person commemorated.

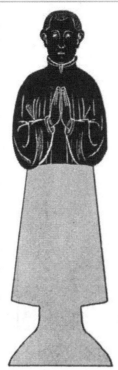

BRASS TO A CIVILIAN, ABOUT 1450.

Next, a Richard Haddock, son of John is listed (1480-1538).

xxiii. jour d'Octobr l'an de Grace m. ccc. lxi : Dieu de lour almes eit mŕci. Though still in Norman-French, which was entirely

Brass of Richard and John Haddock and families, 1453, at Leigh.

discarded soon after in favour of Latin, this inscription gives, as will be seen, much more information than those given above, including the date of death.

At Leigh, near Southend, there is a fine brass, still perfect in all its parts, though rather battered, which well depicts the civilian costume of the middle of the fifteenth century. Its date is 1453, and it commemorates Richard Haddock, of Leigh, his two wives, Christina and Margaret (apparently represented by a single effigy), their seven sons and three daughters; also John Haddock, son of the above, with his wife, Alice, and their eight sons and three daughters.

Then, as we find Richard's son, Robert Haddock listed, the picture becomes clearer with more sources and many family trees coming together in the picture. It seems they all lived in the same area, thus making it more plausible that they were related.

On a modern map, you will find the city of Chelmsford located just Northeast from the greater London area. (The reliquary and illustrated archaeologist, 1895)

<u>Leigh, a seaport city</u>

Early historical records show the Haddocks in Leigh, a parish of Lancashire, England located at the mouth of the Thames River. They were a self-sufficient family, constructing boats with precision and venturing forth on bays and firths to bring in loads of fish for barter. Over the years, they fished and sold their products up and down the coasts. They married in various places until the name Haddock could be found in Scotland, Wales and Ireland, as well as England.

In 1564, the historian Camden described Leigh as "*a proper fine little towne and verie full of stout and adventurous sailers.*" -(Camden, 1551-1623). The riverside settlement of 'Old Leigh', (also regarded colloquially as 'the old town'), was historically significant, situated as it was along the primary shipping route to London. From the middle Ages until the turn of the twentieth-century, Old Leigh provided a market square and hosted the village's earlier high street. Leigh had grown to become a prosperous port by the 16th century, ships as large as 340 tons were built here for fishing and other purposes. By the late 19th century however, Leigh's deep water access had become silted up, and the village began to decline in importance as an anchorage and port of call.

The main seafood catch from Leigh fishing boats has always been shellfish and whitebait. Many of the local trawlers were at one time bawleys, and two of Old Leigh's pubs - the *Peter Boat* and *Ye Olde Smack*- owe their names to types of local fishing boat, (peter boat, smack). Local fish merchants land, process and trade a wide range of supplies daily, including shrimps, lobster, crab, seabass, haddock, cod and mackerel, cockles, whelks, mussels and oysters.

With the advent of the railway line from London to Southend during the mid-19th century, much of 'the old town' was demolished to accommodate its passage, and new housing and streets began to be built upon the ridge of hills above the settlement. (The current railway station is situated near the western end of old Leigh's cockle sheds and boat marina, replacing in 1936 the original station, which was situated opposite Bell Wharf.) (From Wikipedia, the free encyclopedia)

On a present-day map, you will find Leigh-on-the sea shown as Southend-on-Sea. It is northeast of Gravesend across from the Thames River and south of Chelmsford.

Focus: Robert Haddock (1525-1571)

Here's what we know about **Robert** Haddock (1525-1571): He seems to have been married twice, once briefly to Elizabeth DRAKE, then to Margaret POWELL, with who he had all his children that we know about. Family tree records are more plentiful for this time and the sources are better since more work has been done by genealogists.

Origins: Seafaring Haddocks

Focus: Richard Haddock, Captain (1559-1660)

We begin well-documented family history with **Richard** Haddock, Robert's son (1559-1660). Richard lived in the same area as Robert and had 2 sons, William and Richard who were apparently captains in the royal navy. Richard Haddock, himself, had been rewarded by the government in 1652, having held commands under both Charles I and subsequently the Parliamentary regime; he commanded the *Victory* in 1642, the *Antelope* in 1643-44, the *John* in 1644 and the *Unicorn* in 1648. In 1652 he served as Vice-Admiral commanding the *Vanguard*.

Here's a quote from an author in the preface of an old text of reproduced church records, that documents the presence of the Haddock family in that area:

> "One name that comes into church registers very early and was perhaps already here when they began is that of Haddock, (for example) a Richard Haddock was parish clerk in the reign of Charles I (1625-1649 about 23 years reign).[by this time, the parish clerk was functioning as an assistant to the church wardens in collecting money for the benefit for the poor as well as other functions. Parish clerks were appointed on the nomination of the parish priest and their tenure was regarded as a freehold (tenured)." (https://en.wikipedia.org/wiki/Parish_(Church_of_England))

"I think the name went on uninterruptedly through that century and the next. He witnessed several marriages in 1655. My published list of Bury Grammar School[2] boys shows six brothers of the name (Haddock) coming to the school from a street in Bury within the first half of the nineteenth century. One of them, a Bedfordshire clergyman, died in 1913 aged 90 years. And now as I am writing this Preface, I see that a sister of theirs, Miss Ann Haddock, brings a long life of 97 years to an end in a house over the way. And with her the long connection of Bury with that name comes to an end. It is curious that an Amy Haddock should have died in June 1825 aged 95 years, as is shown by a stone in the churchyard. The two together make a bridge over a space of 185 years, from George II to George V, from Walpole to Asquith, from Marlborough to Kitchener and French" (Booth, 1916)

I'm not sure if this is the same as our Richard Haddock, but it very well could have been, considering the place and his birth and death dates are within the time range.

In the mid-1500's, the English navy was in the process of re-building and organizing operations from prior wars. Privaterring was permitted by general proclamation with the natural result of encouraging piracy. Anyone related to the royal court were willing to turn a blind eye to piracy if they were given ten percent of the proceeds. This was especially true in wartime, but became a common practice during peace as well. (Rodger, 1997) By 1603, the English Navy Royal was in many respects stronger and more capable than it had been on the outbreak of the Spanish war 20 years before. The ability to keep a ship properly victualled for a fighting force and to finance naval operations through piracy helped grow the merchant fleet to where it was estimated to be 20 times the size of queen Elizabeth's navy. (Rodger, 1997) Therefore, the process of supplying ships with the proper amount of good food, water, and drink went through a bad period during the late 1500's and emerged into the 1600's better organized and less corrupt. It was into this period of improvement in the British Navy that our ancesters emerged.

Captain **William** Haddock, a direct descendant of **Richard**, produced the most famous son, another Richard, who became Admiral of the English navy and was knighted by the king. This marked the highlight of English sea captains.

_____

2 an independent' day school in Bury, Greater Manchester, England, that has existed since c.1570

Focus: William Haddock, Captain (1607-1667)

When William Haddock was born in April 1607 in Essex, his father, Richard, was 25 and his mother, Frances, was 30. He married Mary GOODLAND and they had nine children together. He died on September 22, 1667, in Essex, at the age of 60.

William married Mary Goodland (1602-1688) on April 9, 1629 in London, when he was 22 years old. She was also the offspring of an English sea captain, Capt. William Goodland. Richard, the oldest son, was born in 1629 in Wapping, a district east of London in Middlesex.

Middlesex was a county in southeast England that is now mostly part of Greater London, with small sections in neighboring counties. It was established in the Anglo-Saxon system from the territory of the Middle Saxons. The historic county included land stretching north of the River Thames from 3 miles (5 km) east to 17 miles (27 km) west of the City of London with the rivers Colne and Lea and a ridge of hills as the other boundaries.

William Haddock and his brothers lived in England in 1667, when the British and Dutch were embroiled in a high seas conflict that dragged on for more than 40 years. They fought in the periods 1652-1674 and 1781-1810, for the control of trade routes and colonies. You can imagine the wives were left alone for periods of time while their husbands were 20 years away at sea. This may explain why some Haddocks married more than once, but had no record of divorce or death of their first wife, in some cases. Some probably died in or after childbirth. For others, they most likely were Catholics and divorce wasn't recognized.

During this time, there was inner conflict between royalty and common rule with Oliver Cromwell uniting his country into the Commonwealth of England for a time. In a few years, Cromwell took what Queen Elizabeth started and King James I improved and created a powerful navy, expanding the number of ships and greatly improving organization and discipline. With this, England was ready to challenge the Dutch trade dominance. These conditions probably gave the family an opportunity to distinguish themselves in the navy and rise the ranks. In fact, many people used the sea to rise to a social rank to which they could not otherwise have aspired during this time. (Rodger, 1997)

William died on September 22, 1667 in Essex at age 60.

A system of paying a subsidy to builders of vessels of more than one hundred tons, instituted by Henry VIII and developed by Elizabeth, resulted in eighteen ships, varying in weight from 105 tons to 340 tons, built at Leigh during the Armada period (repulsion of the Spanish Armada). This fact adds to the reputation that the town was a notable port. With that in mind, it is possible that the pilgrim ship "Mayflower" was built at Leigh, though this theory has become less and less popular. (Warwicker, 1973)

Focus: Richard Haddock, Sir Admiral (1629-1715)

Into such a thriving little area was born one **Richard** Haddock, in the year 1629 (note that there were several Richards in the Haddock family and they are often confused. The actual birth dates help keep the genealogy straight). Richard was Captain **William**'s son, the person previously highlighted in this section. Richard grew up at a time when the sea was a veritable challenge to every Englishman. It was not surprising that Richard Haddock distinguished himself in a naval career and was among several captains (and one of two admirals), which the Haddock family gave to the English Navy during the seventeenth and eighteenth centuries, serving for almost 100 years.

Richard Haddock's will shows that he was a well-to-do man possessing land and capital by the time he died. To his children and grandchildren, some of whom had married into other prominent Leigh families, Richard Haddock bequeathed approximately five hundred pounds in money, as well as land. He was evidently a man of some learning for he possessed books which were left to his second wife, Elizabeth HURLESTON. After providing adequately for his family, Richard Haddock made sure of his soul by saying that five pounds was to be distributed to the poor of Leigh as his wife thought fit. (Warwicker, 1973).

Following outstanding service in the first Dutch Wars, then, Captain Richard Haddock became Admiral Haddock and was appointed commissioner of the Navy. On July 3rd, 1675, he was knighted by the King of England, Charles II.

Sir Richard apparently had several children from two marriages. His youngest son from the second marriage, Nicholas, also distinguished himself as a ship captain rising to the rank of admiral in the British Navy (Haddock, 1964). Nicholas, also amassed some wealth, having, having ownership of Wrotham Place at his time of death. (Warwicker, 1973)

As stated, Richard HADDOCK was born in 1629 in Wapping, Middlesex to Mary Goodland and William Haddock.

Richard married (1) Elizabeth "Lydia" WILKINSON, daughter of Henry Wilkinson and Joane Cannon, on 13 February 1648 at St Katharine's by the Tower. They had three children, Jeane (married John Greene in 1672), John (who went to America & connects to the Haddocks in the United States), and Richard. This family is our direct line of ancestors while the second family would be half-relatives since there was a different mother.

The soon to be named, 'Sir Richard' also married (2) Elizabeth HURLESTON, daughter of Adm. Nicholas Hurleston and Anna Moyer, on 24 July 1671 at St Botolph-without-Bishopsgate and had seven children; Martha who married Dennis Lyddoll; Capt. Richard b. abt 1673 - 21 April 1751; William; Elizabeth; Capt. Joseph Haddock; Adm. of the Blue, Nicholas Haddock (1685–1746); Lydia.[9]

Sir Richard's nephew (his brother, William's son), also named Richard, served in the Navy and fought in the first battle of the third Anglo-Dutch war, commanding the fire ship *Anne and Christopher* at the Battle of Solebay, being commended for his bravery. Sir Richard's brother, Joseph Haddock, also had a naval career as a Lieutenant during the Third Anglo-Dutch War, later commanding HMS *Swallow* in 1678. Sir Richard's eldest son (by his second wife), another Richard, followed his father into the Navy and in April 1734 was appointed to his father's old post of Controller of the Navy. Sir Richard's third son, Nicholas, ended a distinguished naval career with the rank of Admiral of the Blue.

Richard HADDOCK (Sir Admiral) lived in England in the mid-1600s when Royalists and Parliamentarians raised arms in one of the bloodiest battles in British history, called the English Civil War.

Sir Richard Haddock (c.1629 – 26 January 1715 was an officer of the Royal Navy. He served during the Anglo-Dutch Wars, eventually rising to the rank of Admiral in August 1690. In Herge's fictional work, Adventures of Tintin, Richard Haddock was one of the inspirations for Captain Haddock's 17th century fictional ancestor, Sir Francis Haddock.

Sir Richard Haddock, Family and early life

As mentioned, Haddock was born into a distinguished navy family. His grandfather, also Richard Haddock, had served in the English navy. His father, William Haddock, also commanded trading vessels, and was appointed on 14 March 1651 to command the *America*, a ship hired by the Commonwealth of

England Navy. He served in the First Anglo–Dutch War and saw action in 1653. For his services, he was awarded a gold medal. William initially lived in Deptford, but subsequently moved to Kent. He had several children, several of whom followed him into the navy, including his son Richard. Also, his maternal grandfather was in the Navy and both grandparents served in naval societies.

Command/Employment

Richard Haddock had command of HMS *Dragon* from 1656 to 1660, but was then unemployed (actually commanded trading vessels between wars) until 1666 when he took command of the 50-gun HMS *Portland* on 14 June 1666. During this period, he was given command of one of the companies involved in the attacks on Ulie and Schelling in August 1666. He relinquished command of the *Portland* on 9 November 1667.

Prior to the outbreak of the Third Anglo-Dutch War in 1672 Haddock became captain of the 100-gun HMS *Royal James* on 18 January of that year; he was her captain at the Battle of Solebay on 28 May. The *Royal James* was the flagship of Admiral Sir Edward Montagu, 1st Earl of Sandwich. The *Royal James* led the van of the Blue Squadron, and attacked Willem Joseph van Ghent's ship. She was then engaged by several other Dutch warships and fire ships. Despite fighting several of them off and forcing Rear-Admiral Jan van Brakel's ship to disengage, the *Royal James* was set on fire by the Dutch. Haddock was wounded in the foot, and on seeing that the ship was doomed, attempted to persuade the Earl to abandon ship. Montagu refused, and Haddock jumped overboard. He survived to be picked up and transferred to another English warship. Montagu was killed in the wreck.

Haddock returned to London and attended a meeting with King Charles II (reigned 1649-1685). There the King bestowed a mark of favor on Haddock for his actions during the battle, taking a satin cap from his head and placing it upon Haddock's. The cap was kept in the family for many years, with a note describing the battle.

Inscription: "This satin cap was given by King Charles the second, in the year 1672, to Sir Richard Haddock, after the English battle with the Dutch, when he had been captain of the Royal James, under the command of the Earl of Sandwich, which ship was burnt, and Sir Richard had been wounded. Given him on his return to London."

Haddock assumed command of the Third rate HMS *Lion* on 7 November 1672, and remained with her until the following 1 February. He was then given command on 2 February 1673 of the brand new First rate HMS *Royal Charles*, flagship of Prince Rupert of the Rhine. He fought at the Battles of Schooneveld on 28 May and 4 June 1673. Immediately following this second action, on 5 June 1673 he was switched to command HMS *Royal Sovereign*, but relinquished command of the *Royal Sovereign* on 30 June, and was quickly appointed to be an Extra Commissioner of the Navy on 18 August 1673.

He was knighted on 3 July 1675. Haddock was appointed Controller of the Navy on 2 February 1682, an appointment he retained until 17 April 1686. He also became commander of HMS *Duke* on 3 June 1682, but this last sea command only lasted 18 days, ending on 21 June. In 1683 he was appointed first Commissioner of the Victualling Office, a post he held until 1690.

Political Life & later offices

He entered politics in 1678, being elected to represent Aldeburg. He became the representative for New Shoreham in 1685, and, just before the accession of King William III, he again became Controller of the Navy on 12 October 1688, a post he held until his death on 29 January 1714. He was appointed joint Commander-in-Chief of the fleet sent to Ireland in 1690, alongside Vice Admiral Henry Killigrew and Sir John Ashby. They commanded the fleet from the third rate HMS Kent. They remained in command until the winter when the fleet returned to Britain. They resigned their commissions and were replaced by Admiral Edward Russell.

Sir Richard was described as 'a man so conversant with the affairs of the navy' that 'the navy would stand still without him'. This was his political importance in the House of Commons. However, he was regarded with intense suspicion by the Whigs, and ordered into custody with Sir John Parsons and his partners after complaints about the 'corrupt and unwholesome victuals' issued to the fleet. 'I must not call it injustice in that august assembly what they did to me', Sir Richard commented bitterly 20 years later, reckoning that it had cost him about £100 in fees to the sergeant-at-arms 'and to lawyers soliciting the House of Commons, with expenses of entertainment whilst in custody'. (Crook, n.d.) Haddock went into retirement from active service, dying in London on 26 January 1715. He was buried at the family seat of Leigh-on-Sea in St Clement Churchyard on 6 February. (http://en,wikipaedia.org/wiki/Richard_Haddock, n.d, n.d.).

1st Marriage

Richard HADDOCK first married Elizabeth "Lydia" WILKINSON in February 1648 in London, London, when he was 19 years old and she must have been about 15. She died around 1670 (conflicting data about her death date) around age 22. *Elizabeth "Lydia" Wilkinson - 1630–1670*

Birth of Children

His daughter Jeane was born in November 1650 in London, London.

His son, John, was born on March 30, 1653, in London, London. *John HADDOCK - 1653–1728*

His son Richard was born on November 22, 1655, in London, London.

Death of Parents

Sir Richard's mother Mary passed away on January 6, 1688, in Essex, at the age of 85.

Sir Richard's father William passed away on September 22, 1667, in Essex, at the age of 60.

Second Marriage

Sir Richard also married (2) Elizabeth HURLESTON, daughter of Adm. Nicholas Hurleston and Anna Moyer, on 24 July 1671 at St Botolph-without-Bishopsgate and had several children.

Birth of Children

His daughter Lydia was born about 1670. *Lydia Haddock - 1670–1732*

His daughter Martha was born in 1672 in London. Martha married Dennis Lyddoll.

Son, Capt. Richard b. abt 1673 - 21 April 1751

His daughter Elizabeth was born in 1683 in London, London. His daughter Elizabeth passed away on February 26, 1709, at the age of 26.

His son Joseph was born on May 8, 1684, in London, who became Capt. Joseph.

Nicholas Haddock (1685–1746); Adm. of the Blue

Occupation

Comptroller of His Majesties Navy, Admiral, politician

Death

Sir Richard HADDOCK died on January 26, 1715, in London, when he was 86 years old.

Summary of Sir Richard's life:

He was married twice and had 2 different sets of children, 3 in the first marriage and 6 in the second. He had a distinguished career in the English Navy rising to the rank of Admiral. His career was not without some conflict, but managed to stay on good terms with the ruling people and out of harm's way until retirement. Ultimately, he was knighted as Sir Richard on 3 July 1675 by Charles II, King of England. (See Appendix I)

In Sir Richard's will, he left to his son, Richard, a house at Mile End and a property in Soham in Cambridgeshire.

Mile End Road is an ancient route from London to the East, and was moved to its present-day alignment after the foundation of Bow Bridge in 1110. In the medieval period, it was known as 'Aldgatestrete', as it led to the eastern entrance to the City of London at Aldgate. The area running alongside Mile End Road was known as Mile End Green, and became known as a place of assembly for Londoners, reflected in the name of Assembly Passage. For most of the medieval period, this road was surrounded by open fields on either side, but speculative developments existed by the end of the 16th century and continued throughout the 18th century. (https://en.wikipedia.org/wiki/Mile_End, n.d.) This may have been the area John Wesley, Methodist evangelist referred to as Aldersgate.

Therefore, available information of the Haddock family in the British Isles tells us they were primarily involved in shipbuilding, fishing and sailing the seas. Several Haddocks apparently distinguished themselves in service of the King's Navy as Captains and two became Admirals.

This was a tumultuous time for monarchs in England, primarily due to religious dissention between the Catholics and Protestants. No monarch reigned between the execution of Charles I in 1649 and the Restoration of Charles II in 1660. Instead, from 1653, the following individuals held power as Lords Protector, during the period known as the Protectorate, when the monarchy was overthrown: Oliver Cromwell and Richard Cromwell. Although the monarchy was restored in 1660, no stable settlement proved possible until the Glorious Revolution of 1688, when Parliament passed legislation prohibiting Roman Catholics from succeeding to the throne. After that it was James II, Mary II, and then William III around the turn of the century. Miraculously, the Haddock family seemed to remain on good terms with the country's various rulers. Through this period, the English Navy achieved a reasonably permanent and effective form of sea power, including the core of a standing state navy. (Rodger, 1997)

Personal note: Along with my wife, Celia, we visited England back in 1999 and while there, I visited the English Maritime Museum. While there, they were having an exhibit on Peter the Great, Russian Tsar, highlighting his visit to England 1697-98. He was still a young man at the time and reportedly traveled to study new developments in technology, especially shipbuilding. He lived in the home of the writer, John Evelyn, for much of his four-month stay in England.

Although officially meant to be travelling incognito, most people seemed to know Peter's identity. At a height of six feet seven, it would have been hard for him to blend into the crowd.

Apparently, he was invited by William III, the king of England at the time (and co-ruler with Mary II). King William welcomed the opportunity to increase trade with Russia, so he gave Peter every assistance he could. By impressing the Tsar, William hoped to win back some of the privileges English merchants had enjoyed in earlier times. The King was especially keen to sell tobacco, grown in the British colony of Virginia, to Russia. During Peter's stay in England, a group of London merchants and financiers gave him thousands of pounds for the right to import tobacco into Russia.

In England Peter met with King William III, visited Greenwich and Oxford, was painted by Sir Godfrey Kneller, and saw a Royal Navy Fleet Review at Deptford. He traveled to the city of Manchester to learn the techniques of city-building, which he would later use to great effect at Saint Petersburg.

Peter's visit was cut short in 1698, when he was forced to rush home by a rebellion of the Streltsy. The rebellion was, however, easily crushed before Peter returned home from England; of the Tsar's troops, only one was killed. Peter nevertheless acted ruthlessly towards the mutineers. Over 1,200 of the rebels were tortured and executed, and Peter ordered that their bodies be publicly exhibited as a warning to future conspirators.[14] The Streltsy were disbanded, and the individual they sought to put on the Throne—Peter's half-sister Sophia—was forced to become a nun. (Peter the Great, n.d.)

One can only imagine how exciting it was for Sir Richard to have served under kings of England, the Parliament, and eventually to possibly meet the Tsar of Russia.

17th Century England

Sir Richard Haddock lived in England during the Gin craze, a time when large amounts of gin were consumed by citizens. For example, the average Londoner consumed 14 gallons of gin each year. The Haddock ancestors continued to leave their mark on English society even after the 'glory days' of the seafaring Haddocks. Let's take a brief look at how the drama played out.

SIN, SMUGGLING & THE METHODIST CHURCH

Throughout the centuries smuggling was, of course, a very lucrative pastime in coastal towns around England. The business of protecting the coastlines and catching smugglers was also lucrative. For the men of nearby Rye southwest of Leigh, in Leigh itself, and, particularly, in the center of the old town in the Customs House, re-built in 1815, there was much work. Even before, there had been a Customs House there and, when it burned, another was re-built. In 1781 a sale at the Customs House of contraband items and boats seized included 680 gallons of gin, 82 gallons of brandy, 47 gallons of rum, 275 quarts of port, 120 quarts of claret, 33 yards of calico, much foreign china and a sloop and small sailing boat. By 1802 the Customs Officer noted that he had made a seizure every day in the month of July.

Between wars, the Haddock seafaring men found work in what amounted to the Coast Guard. Called cutters, they commanded ships who searched for smugglers and provided protection for the smaller ships that hauled the recovered goods, back up the Thames River. Some recovered goods were routed back to sailors who worked on the ships (through the victualling process). The sailors who were captured were forced into the service of the English Navy. As the result, the Captains received about 500 pounds each, which helped make them wealthy, in those days.

We know, John Wesley, founder of the Methodist religion, paid frequent visits to the quaint old towns of Rye, Leigh, and neighborhoods in between. Between the years 1758 and 1790, he visited Leigh 6 times. He told a friend how the folk there were very poor and on one occasion a dirty destitute woman came knocking at the door of where he was staying in the old town begging for food for her many children. John Wesley went on to say how poverty stricken the area was at the time of his visits. When he set up the new Methodist worshipping group in the old town of Leigh it was the first of its kind in Essex and fishermen went out from Leigh to spread the gospel all over the county. In the 19th century a Methodist Minister of Leigh described the inhabitants like this: "the fishermen I came into contact with at Leigh were old men with no scholarship."

There was at that time a wealthy Haddock family living in Rye. (Wesley Historical Society). Old Captain William Haddock, the patriarch, was commander of "The Stag" revenue cutter (ship) in the Customs Service (Coast Guard). He married Miss Ann Bray in 1759, and they were the parents of three sons and three daughters. He died July 29, 1812, aged 75, buried in Rye Church.

This line of Haddocks has not been documented as descendants, but the stories are worth mentioning. Surely, they are related. For those wanting to research further, here is a story and additional family notes:

Captain John Haddock's sister, Ann, married Lewis Meryon (of Huguenot descent) in 1765. They had children: John, Sarah, Charles Lewis and Thomas. Sarah married William Holloway. Beside John and Ann, Capt. William Haddock's children other than John and Ann were: Joseph and Henry.

The rest of the story begins with Henry:

Their eldest son, Henry, was also a Captain in the Customs Service. He had been brought up a churchman, but having attended Methodist services, became impressed with their earnestness of spirit, and there he met Miss Lisa Barnes and fell in love with her! He made her an offer of marriage, which she at first declined. Captain Haddock was a gallant young fellow, and did not give up. He became an out-and-out Christian, and joined the Methodist Society. Miss Barnes, when she saw a real change in his life, consented to the marriage. They furnished a house and were preparing for the wedding, when all their happy hopes were dashed to the ground.

It seems that Captain Henry Haddock, while commanding his vessel between Dover and Dunkirk, spied a smuggling craft in the distance, and on approaching, before they could hail her, the crew of the stranger fired at Captain Henry Haddock's vessel. He ordered his men not to fire, but they inadvertently did, upon which, the smugglers fired their big guns. A ball came through the upper part of the vessel, passing through the thigh, body and right arm of Captain Haddock. He was just heard to moan, and expired immediately in the arms of one of his crew on August 19, 1783, at the early age of eighteen.

The sad circumstances connected with the death of Captain Henry Haddock so affected his brother John, that on the evening of the interment he decided to devote all his powers to God's service. He, too, was smitten with the charms of Miss Barnes, which ultimately resulted in their marriage on June 12, 1786. It is said that the dowry consisted of her actual weight in gold.

It is said, John Haddock was a successful merchant. He entered business, not for his own necessities, but solely that he could more generously assist the poor and needy. He was deservedly respected by all his fellow townsmen for the unspotted purity of his character, his wisdom in counsel, and his great liberality and kindness of heart. One instance might be mentioned amongst many. A party of soldiers in March called at Rye to rest on their journey, and filled all the inns. It being wet and cold, many of the poor women and children were almost perishing. As soon as Mr. Haddock heard of their distressing circumstances he hastened to their relief, and his house found room for about fifty of them, who were gratuitously accommodated during their stay.

Until this time, the Methodists had worshipped in the old Presbyterian chapel on Mermaid Street (the Presbyterians originated in Scotland). In January, 1788, John Haddock, seeing the need of a new chapel to accommodate the increasing congregations, purchased a house and piece of ground in Badding's Ward from the descendants of Samuel Burt. The ground was formerly a part of the old churchyard.

John Haddock pulled down the house and built a chapel, and minister's residence "at his own expense" John Wesley (1703-1791) opened the new chapel on Wednesday, January 28, 1789. He records the fact in his journal, and remarks: "It is a noble building, much loftier than most of our houses, and finely situated at the head of the town. It was thoroughly filled. Such a congregation I never saw at Rye before; which, added to the peaceable, loving spirit they are now in, gives reason to hope there will be such a work here as has not been heretofore." (Wesley, Vol. IV, p. 426)

At this time, Mr. and Mrs. Haddock were residing, during the winter months, in High Street, Rye. It was here they entertained John Wesley. The summer months were spent at Tanhouse, 7 Northiam. The house is still standing. It is a picturesque 16th century black and white timber structure, situated on the southern border of the parish.

This story takes on greater significance as the history of the Haddocks in the New World unfolds as John Wesley visited the region of Georgia in the United States, near where one branch of the Haddocks migrated.

PART II

Linkage with American Haddocks

There was an oral tradition in the American Haddock family genealogy that they were descended from the Leigh Haddocks, although until recent history with internet connections, there was no easy access to documentary evidence to confirm the tradition. For many years, a belief existed in the family that their ancestor was a famous English admiral, and amongst the early eighteenth century settlers were namesakes of the Leigh Haddocks.

It was no surprise to find a member of the Leigh Haddock family had settled in the New World for they were known to be adventurous and sea-loving. In October, 1648, one William Haddocke, "a planter of Virginia," died abroad; Richard Haddocke, his brother, was his executor and benefactor of the will. His will is originally signed October 4, 1648 and recorded in Fairfax, Virginia dated, 1649. Apparently the will was sent to London where it was probated August 27, 1649 to Richard Haddock, girdler (a belt maker or livery equipment maker, like harness). Presently, a direct connection has yet to be made with this person, but he is the first documented Haddock in the new world. It's doubtful it was the same Richard's family.

The Earl of Warwick (not sure which one), with whom Sir Richard Haddock was friends, had financial interests in the New World colonies. The fact that no documents (until recently) relating to the Leigh Haddocks mention relatives abroad could be for a few reasons. There may have been a quarrel in the family, a member of the family may have been disgraced, there may have been a family dispute between heirs of Sir Richard's 2 sets of kids, or the Haddock adventurer may have been a very distant relative who left for the Americas in the early 1600's (Warwicker, 1973).

Historical Evidence

A bit of history supports this last possibility. Up to the 1550's, at least, Scottish seamen were well in advance of the English. They regularly made long open sea passages, while the English remained tied to coastal waters. (Rodger, 1997) In 1607, King James VI of Scotland, who had also become King James I of England, decided to send an expedition to the New World to bring back masts for ships. The timber in Scotland was very scrubby with few trees large enough to make good masts. The king resolved to enlarge the Navy of Scotland and England, a project which required good masts to do so.

What the legends say

Legends in the Haddock family tell us that four Haddock brothers of Scotland signed up for the expedition. Reaching the New World, they were entranced by the deep forests of the Massachusetts Territory, the waters teeming with fish and the game that was so abundant. They resolved to return with their own ship as soon as they were able.

When the Haddock brothers arrived back in the British Isles, they immediately began their preparations. In 1610, they made their way back to Massachusetts Territory with their own ship and supplies.

It was late autumn when they arrived on the shores of the New World and an early winter had gripped the land. The weather was terrible but they managed to land on the Maine shore of what is now the Piscataqua River, between the present towns of Portsmouth, New Hampshire and South Berwick, Maine. In the manner of Haddocks, who are not given to fancy words, they named the place "The Landing."

Unable to fall timber in the howling storms, they dug a cellar, lined with large stones and settled down for the winter. The four men had plenty of supplies and managed to survive the bitter weather.

As spring came on, they worked up and down the coast gathering marketable timber and fish, but they did not make a permanent settlement. Yet, they always returned to "The Landing" and thought of it fondly as their first home in the New World. "The Landing" was so much a part of their thoughts and traditions that, generations later, Charles Haddock, Sr., in faraway Missouri, exacted from his son, Charles, Jr., a promise that someday he would go and stand on 'The Landing,' where our people first entered the New World. Young Charles failed in his promise, but exacted the same promise from his son, Ransom Haddock. Ransom, too, was unable to keep the promise, but his granddaughter, Alma (Haddock) Martin, at last fulfilled the promise by going back to the spot near South Berwick, Maine, around the turn of the century (1900's) and standing on "The Landing" as her grandfather had requested. She also found the cellar hole still in existence and a burying ground with graves of early day Haddocks. Instead of tombstones, some of the graves were covered with slabs of slate with names on them that seemed to have been roughly carved with a knife. (Haddock H. R., 1976)

She reported that at least two were legible: Ezra Haddock and his wife, Ida Earle. (//www.seacoastnh.com/History/As-I-Please/did-haddocks-settle-maine-in-1610/)

Personal note: To attempt to further document the connection to the Maine Haddocks, I also visited South Berwick, Maine in 1991. There I found a quiet New England village located near the southern border of New Hampshire where the shipbuilding and seaport cities of Portsmouth and Kittery are located. I also located a spot in South Berwick referred to as the Landing. In further investigation, I learned that the original Landing was probably located downstream about a quarter of a mile or so and it was presently unmarked. There was no evidence of gravestones and no local historical records of any early Haddock gravesites. In addition, there was no recorded histories of any early Haddocks living in the area. This supports the oral tradition that the Haddocks visited this area very early (before documented history of the area) and moved on down the coast before any permanent settlements were established.

Legend has it that these early Haddock brothers constructed boats and ships and reportedly built one ship named the 'May Flower.' A 'May Flower' was registered in Scarborough in 1630 with Robert Haddock as Master. The registry of this ship is noted in "The Mayflower and Log" by Ames as one of the many ships built with that name from the late 1500's through mid-1600's.

Family legends also tell us that a few years after the arrival of the Haddock brothers in the Massachusetts Territory, two of them brought their families from Scotland. This was prior to the coming of the Pilgrims and an expression often heard in the Haddock family is the quip, "Our family didn't come over in the Mayflower. They were on hand to greet it when it arrived." This was indeed true if the legend can be believed.

The first house built by the Haddock brothers in Maine was a long, low shed constructed over the cellar hole where they spent their first winter. It had no windows, but had strong doors, one on either end of the building. It was ideal for storage while they were away.

From a book on the local history, it was evident from the town records that wolves were the greatest problem for the early settlers. Apparently, the Indians were friendly and accustomed to encountering white people who traveled in and out of the area. However, the wolves continued to be a serious problem until the end of the 18th century (Banks, 1990).

In the beginning, the brothers hauled the products they gathered to Scotland and England but as time went on they became a part of the developing coastal trade between the colonies. The families grew and prospered. They probably settled further down the coast but later returned to the vicinity of South Berwick, Maine. It was reported that in 1970 Haddocks were still to be found in the little town of South Berwick. One name was still listed in the phone book when I visited in 1991; a Samuel Haddock.

We now know that our line of Haddocks originated from England, not Scotland, and migrated to Virginia and Maryland. Therefore, we honor the legends by assuring this was another group of ancestors that may have been related.

What the historians say: The Mayflower

As we all know, the Mayflower was the ship that carried the first Pilgrims to America in 1620. It was built around 1610 and probably looked like other ships of its time, which had three masts and two decks. It probably measured about 90 feet long and weighed about 180 short tons. Its quarter-owner, Thomas Jones, served as master.

The Mayflower sailed from Plymouth, England, on September 16, 1620, with 120 passengers. The ship reached the Cape Cod coast 66 days after it left England and dropped anchor off what is now Provincetown Harbor on November 21, 1620. It reached the present-day site of Plymouth, Massachusetts on December 26, five days after a small party had explored the site and decided to make Plymouth their new home.

From the book, "The Mayflower and Log" by Ames, we learn that there was a 'sleight-of-hand trick; involved in that expedition to the new world. It seems that Thomas Jones, the master (or captain) of the Mayflower, was without doubt the old servant of Lord Warwick (the 2nd Earl of Warwick), having done his 'dirty work' for years and had been paid off by Lord Warwick and Sir Ferdinando Georges to steal the Pilgrim colony from the London Virginia Company and hand it over to the their company (Warwick & Georges) simply by landing the Pilgrims in New England instead of northern Virginia, as planned. By the time the Pilgrims got to America, they were ready to set up homestead anywhere on land, without concern if it was located above or below the 41st parallel of north latitude. So, it was easy for captain Jones to manipulate the Pilgrims to establish a colony in New England because they just wanted off the ship. This small adjustment meant a difference in fortunes for Warwick and Georges.

Sir Ferdinando Gorges, (born about 1656 & died 1647) is thought to be the proprietary founder of Maine, while the 2nd Earl of Warwick (1587-1658) is credited as founding the colony of Rhode Island in 1644. Warwick was one of the most powerful landowners in England and financed several expeditions. Both had roots in the Essex area and had held positions in the English Navy, although Warwick never actually went to America. Also, both were thought to have had connections to the seafaring Haddocks during those times.

The Mayflower left America on April 5, 1621. Historians are not certain what happened to the ship after it returned to England. Some believe it was dismantled after Jones died in 1622, although a ship called the Mayflower made trips to America after that. Others believe that William Russell bought the Mayflower for salvage, and used its hull as a barn roof. The barn stands in Jordans, a village outside London (The World Book Encyclopedia, 1979b).

Evidence of European visits and occupancy of the Maine coast has been drowned out by the stories of the Pilgrims and Puritans, who would have us believe that U.S. history began with the Mayflower. Long before the Mayflower, the Maine coast was known intimately by the adventurous navigators of France and Spain. It was also well known to the early English explorers in the 16th century as a place whose beginnings ran back indefinitely. This is also evidenced by several accounts that the Maine Indians spoke broken English and French. They were also mentioned as wearing particles of European clothing and possessing metal implements apparently given them by previous visitors. During these early times, the South Berwick area was used as a "Landing" for several expeditions, which were mostly looking for sassafras, one of the prime objects of every voyage. When unable to find the desired herbs, the expeditions continued their search further down the southern coastline (Banks, 1990).

What the historians say: Maine

It is generally accepted that Vikings, led by Leif Ericson, probably visited Maine about A.D. 1000. Many historians believe that John Cabot, an Italian sea captain in the service of England, reached Maine in 1498. France sent many explorers to Maine. These explorers and the dates they reached Maine included Giovanni da Verrazano (1524), Pierre du Guast, Sieur de Nibts (1604), and Samuel de Champlain (1604). Champlain explored and named Mount Desert, the largest island along Maine's coast.

In 1605, Sir Fernando Gorges and Sir John Popham, two wealthy Englishmen, sent George Waymouth to explore the Maine coast. Waymouth's favorable reports about the area led Gorges and Popham to attempt a settlement in Maine. In 1607, they financed a group of colonists who established Popham Plantation, near the mouth of the Kennebec River. Cold weather and other hardships forced the settlers to return to England in 1608. While in Maine, the settlers built a boat called the Virginia. It was the first boat built by English colonists in America. Perhaps the first permanent settlement was made near present-day Saco in 1623 (Encyclopedia, 1979b). The English made many settlements in Maine during the early 1620's and by then, Sir Gorges, with 30 years' experience, solidly had his hand in New England affairs back in England.

Alexander Brown, who has written several books on the early history of New England, says that the banks of New England were fished from the year 1540 on and in the year 1600, there were some 200 English ships and'10,000 English men and boys' fishing the grand banks. Brown estimated the permanent population of Maine in 1620 at 500. This was before the coming of the Puritans. (Brown, 1898)

More legends

The migration of the Haddocks from Maine to North Carolina has not been traced exactly, but it is almost certain to have been by water, as travel by water was much easier and safer than travel by land. Legend suggests that "one of the brothers went south to care for that end of business." Historical records reflect how fish were caught along the New England coast and barreled for sale in the South. This trade reached as far as the West Indies. On return voyages, ships carried such things as molasses, rum, tar, turpentine, and tobacco. The Haddocks were almost certain to have been involved in the shipping and trade business due to their experience with the merchant marines and victualling.

With this travel going on all the time between New England and the Southern Colonies, relatives would have found it easy to visit one another in the years before the Revolutionary War. However, while the war was in progress, shipping became extremely dangerous and ties between families in the North and South were severed.

In harmony with stories of the nationality of the Haddocks, a great number of them reportedly still carried the reddish hair suggesting a Scottish or Irish ancestry. Others were dark and family legends tell us the Haddocks were also part Delaware Indian (Haddock & Haddock, undated), although there is no documented proof. 1979a). Further, there is family legend and some documentation that some Haddocks married into the Cherokee tribe.

Other Evidence of Haddocks in the New England area:

Besides the current residence of a Samuel Haddock in the South Berwick, Maine area, additional evidence was found of Haddocks in the New England area later in the 1770's and 1800's. For example, a Roger Haddock was listed as having joined the Revolutionary forces in Suffolk County,

Massachusetts in March 1, 1779. In addition, a Jacob Haddock and Levina Foss announced their marriage intentions on July 30, 1846 in Stratham, New Hampshire. Finally, there was a Watson J. Haddock who lived in the area around 1872 and records indicate he was born in Warwick, a province of Quebec, Canada. He was the son of Jacob Haddock and Mary Ann Watson. This suggests that Haddocks may have moved north up the coastline as well as south down the coastline. It should also be remembered that a William Haddocke, planter from Virginia, died abroad in 1648, as mentioned earlier in this chapter. This suggests that Haddocks also settled in Virginia and southern Maryland, and only recently has been documented. Also, there is an island off the coast of Lincoln County, Maine called Haddock Island, but it's probably named after the codfish, which is prevalent in the area.

History of English Immigration to America in the 1600's

Why did people want to leave England and why did they want to move to America? The reasons for the English Immigration to America was at first based on obtaining profit from the new lands but quickly changed as people decided to move from England to escape religious and political prosecution. The prospect of a new life and owning some land was also a major reason for the English immigration to America. Although there were a couple of 'false starts', English Immigration to America continued as thousands of English people undertook 'The Great Migration' between 1620 and 1640. Immigration to America led to the establishment of the first 13 Colonies. It is estimated that over 50,000 undertook the 3000-mile journey to America during the Great Migration. In 1642, the English Civil War (1642–1651) erupted and it is estimated that up to 10% of the English migrants returned to England to fight on the Puritan side. Therefore, I have attempted to identify members of the Haddock family who migrated and stayed in America as reported in their place of death.

The Headright System

Immigration to America substantially increased with the introduction of the Headright System in 1691. Headrights were granted by the London Virginia company giving 50 acres of land to colonists who paid their own way to Virginia, or paid the way for someone else to go. The prospect of owning land, an impossible dream in England, was a great incentive for English Immigration to America and enjoy the opportunities offered in the 'New World'. This idea of granting land to settlers as an incentive came from the Romans and was carried over all the way to Texas when that area was being settled.

The English Bill of Rights

The immigration to America steadily increased as events occurring in England had a significant impact on the migrant. For example, the Glorious Revolution which resulted in the English Bill of Rights being passed in 1689 gave the individual clearly stated rights. Elements of the English Bill of Rights and the earlier Magna Carta would later feature in the American Declaration of Independence of 1776 and in the U.S. Constitution. (http://www.emmigration.info/english-immigration-to-america.htm, n.d.)

Several Haddocks were living near the Virginia/Maryland border in the late 1600's and early 1700's. Birth dates are used to distinguish individuals since many were named similarly.

1648 – William Haddocke, a planter in Fairfax, Virginia died and left a will and estate to his brother, Richard.

1671 - John I Haddock (1653-1728) our direct relative, was the oldest son of Sir Richard Haddock (1629-1715) and Elizabeth "Lydia" Wilkinson, referred to as 'the son who went to America'. Records show him migrating in 1671 to Virginia, the year after his mother died. It looks like he was about 18 when he migrated. This would make him the Pathfinder of the family. If this is the same relative who arrived this early, there are very little records until he shows up in Maryland at a much later age.

1678 – Thomas Haddock (1640-1703) and his sister, Jane Haddock, children of Richard Haddock (1614-1673) and Frances Adye migrated to Maryland. Thomas Haddock/Huddock was transported into the colony of Maryland as a servant in 1678. (Skordas*:200 - WC2:24 &106), apparently by Marke Corder, who was granted 450 acres for transporting nine persons into the Province in 1678--list includes Thomas Haddock. (Harrington* :2 - Patents WC2:106) Thomas married Mary Doxey and had 4 children, one being a James Haddock, who may have been a Colonel in the Revolutionary War.

1685 – Benjamin Haddock (1635-1703), son of Captain Richard Haddock (1581-1660), migrated in 1685 along with his son, James and 3 daughters, shortly after his wife died Records show he owned land on the east side of the Potomac. In that area, there is a place referred to as the 'Haddock Hills'.

1696 – Cornelius Haddock (1612-1696), older brother of Benjamin (above), migrated in 1696 and apparently died the same year at age 84.

1701 - James Haddock (1651-1731), Benjamin's son. James was in St. Georges' County practicing law. There are some land records referencing James and his wife, Sarah Marsham. She was ¼ Piscataway Indian and was married at least 3 times. Each time she seemed to have increased her wealth, as shown by deeds and wills recorded at the time. In the land records, he was referred to as a priest, probably an Anglican.

For example, this is how the records reported her marriages and gives the reader an idea how dates were estimated when there were no actual records (marriage, birth, etc.): "1. Sarah Marsham was born in Calvert County, Maryland, say about 1667, married first Basil Waring say about 1685, married second William Barton after December 29, 1688, married third James Haddock after April 19, 1703, and died in Charles County, Maryland, after January 8, 1733."

"The approximate year of Sarah's marriage to Basil Waring is estimated from the year of Basil's death preceded by four years to account for the births of two children. see Will of Basil Waring, signed December 8, 1688, probated December 29, 1688, Maryland Calendar of Wills, Vol. 2, p. 50, and Liber 6, Folio 66. Basil named his wife Sarah and sons Marsham and Basil. The terminus a quo (limit from which—earliest possible date) for Sarah's marriage to William Barton is determined by the probate date of the will of her first husband Basil Waring. See Will of Basil Waring, signed December 8, 1688, probated December 29, 1688, Maryland Calendar of Wills, Vol. 2, p. 50, and Liber 6, Folio 66. The terminus a quo (limit from which—earliest possible date) for Sarah's death is determined by her deed to Robert Mackhorn. See Deed from Sarah Haddock to Robert Mackhorn, signed January 8, 1733, recorded March 18, 1733/4, Charles County Land Records: 1733-1743, Book O #2, page 28. "Sarah Haddock, widow, of Prince George's County, formerly wife of William Barton, late of Charles County, Gent., deceased, to Robert Mackhorn of Charles County, planter. William Barton by his will, divised to his son-in-law, Basil Waring, 300 acres, being part of this tract of land called Hadlow, lying in Charles County, and the rest of Hadlow to his wife, being now the aforementioned Sarah Haddock. Now this deed witnesses that sd. Sarah Haddock, for 4500 lbs. tobacco, has sold to …. the division line made by sd. Sarah Haddock and Basil Waring. Signed Sarah Haddock. Wit. Jas. Haddock Waring, Henry Keen." Note: (TOBACCO was traded equally as money.) But

There are also records of James Haddock, being a member of the bar in Prince George County and serving as Sheriff from 1716-1719, as a justice (of the peace) 1826, and foreman of the grand jury during 1742-43. The lucrative office of sheriff was considered the most important office of the county and was much sought after. The sheriff received 10 per cent of the annual levy for collecting it, plus certain fees. The Bar of Prince George's was the largest and the most distinguished in the Western Shore counties. There was a half dozen members known throughout the whole province: James Haddock, was listed among them. (HORN, 1976) In that same publication, there was a John Haddock admitted to practice law on June 24, 1701. The dates match and we are assuming this is our John I, James' cousin.

Even then, it was much about who you knew. Mr. James Haddock was married to the widow of Major William Barton, thus becoming the stepfather of Basil Waring and the stepfather-in-law of John Murdock and Samuel Perrie, all who were heavily involved in the politics of that time and place. (Hienton, unknown)

To sum it up, Sir Richard had several relatives who we now know migrated to the United States. All the birth dates match and family tree connections double-checked, but there still is much room for error. It appears that john haddock lived and worked in both Prince George county and Charles county.

Separating fact from fiction

Remember that legends are just that and legends do not contain proof but are honored by genealogists because they must carry enough weight to be repeated over generations. Another family researcher, Gerald 'Jerry' Haddock, of Illinois wrote in 1993 about the need for further study of the early history of New England. He quotes from Charles M Andrews' book called *The Colonial Period of American History,* "…region from Piscataqua to Casco Bay was occupied by a very different type of settler from that which accompanied Winthrop to Massachusetts …seamen and adventurers, who cared for nothing about theological dogmas and church reform… as a rule, of the landed gentry, loyalist in sympathy and adherents of the Anglican Church, with nothing in common with Puritanism. The body of the people were, like their forbearers, sturdy, coarse, hard-drinking, profane, none too fond of the Church, and impatient of too strict an enforcement of law and order." (Andrews, 1934, p 428)

It may be helpful to think of the first wave of Haddock visitors to the Americas as adventurers or pathfinders, while the ones who came and stayed in the colonies, as settlers. Either way, we now have documented connections, relatives who seem to connect the old world with the new world. That person is a **John Haddock**, who was born in England and died in Maryland. Here's what that word and no one will warn we know about him:

Focus: John I Haddock (1653-1728)

When **JOHN I** Haddock was born on March 30, 1653, his father, Sir Richard, was 23 and his mother, Elizabeth, was 22. Birth 30 Mar 1653, London, Middlesex, England. He, Richard, would later be knighted and named Admiral of the British Navy. Will and that Acton

JOHN Haddock was born on March 30, 1653, to Elizabeth "Lydia" Wilkinson, age 22, and Richard HADDOCK, age 23

Baptism

30 Mar 1653, St Bartholomew by the Exchange, London,

Immigration

In 1671-1672 records show a John Haddock on the passenger list of immigrates arriving in Virginia at 18. A history of that location reported that few settlers chose to settle in the area of the county until the early 1700s, because the region was the scene of the bloodiest fighting and slaughters in the Indian wars. (Prince William County Virginia, 2016)

This son, John, referred to as the son 'who went to America', was not listed in his father's will. He may have immigrated due to religious reasons, or he may have been left out of his father's will, especially after his father re-married, or, simply may have sought a better life. If John immigrated at 18, then he may have lost touch with his dad and/or family and his whereabouts may have not been known when his dad died. Many people left England during these times seeking religious freedom and Maryland, where he had children and died, was predominately Catholic.

Much is unknown about John I's life. Other than the migration to Virginia, which was just across the Potomac River from St. Mary's, in Maryland, he first shows up in records obtaining his approval to practice law in Maryland. He was older and may have other marriages. Therefore, more may be revealed about his life in Virginia during the period from immigration to the marriage in Maryland. This would be another area of study for the serious researcher.

Religion

Religious freedom could have been a reason for John's migration. Many Haddocks were victuallers by trade. In 1692, a John Haddock refused to take the oath of fidelity (to English crown?) and listed as a reputed papist (loyal to Pope) in parish of St. James, Westminster. Also, listed as a victualler, probably supplying to the English Navy, on Sherwood St. 27 Jun 1692 Middlesex County, England. This is probably not the same John Haddock, since we think ours had already immigrated to America.

Occupation

In Prince George County, Maryland, a John Haddock was admitted to practice law on June 24, 1701. Since James Haddock, his cousin, was already well-known in this county, it is assumed this is our John I. These were the beginnings of the bar in Maryland and at this time, they could qualify by either of two methods. They could present evidence that they were members of the Inns of Court or Chancery in London, or they could submit to an examination by the Governor and Council (HORN, 1976).

Marriage

JOHN Haddock married Elizabeth ABELL in 1716 in St Mary's City, Maryland, when he was 63 years old. Her family had arrived in the Americas early and she was settled as a second-generation colonist. She was between 39 and 40 years old at the time. She and her family of origin had been in the United States for quite some time before he arrived and several of them fought in the Revolutionary War against the British. http://person.ancestry.com/tree/44543986/person/6217508041 Elizabeth Abell - 1677–1750

Birth of Children

His son John G Haddock, hereafter referred to as John II, was born in 1720 in St Mary's City, Maryland when he was about 67. *John II G HADDOCK Jr.- 1720–1809*

1720 St Mary's, St Mary's County, MD, USA

His son William was born in 1725 in St Mary's City, Maryland when he, John I, was about 68.

William Haddock - 1725–1764

1725 St Mary's, St Mary's County, MD, USA

Death

John I Haddock died in 1728 in St Mary's County, Maryland, when he was 75 years old. He is buried in Trinity Church Cemetery along with many of the Abells and other early settlers, including Leonard Calvert, the first governor of Maryland.

Summary of John I's life:

John I really looks like an adventurer of a different breed when you review his life: born in England, migrated to America around age 18, and died in Maryland where he married and raised 2 sons.

There is a high probability that he was Catholic since many British subjects immigrated for religious reasons and ended up in Maryland.

We don't know much about his life in adulthood until he shows up in the records just before marrying. It's possible that he traveled back and forth between England and America during the early years of his life. We can assume that he was educated because in 1701, he was admitted to practice law in Prince George County, where his brother, James, also practiced.

When he married, his wife was much younger and came from a family already established in Maryland. (See Appendix II)

The following are additional clues to the nature of his life in New England: (also see Appendix II)

1728 Saint Mary's County, MD, USA

> The following looks like settlements recorded in the state of Maryland upon the death of John I Haddock:

> 14.84 SM £14.7.3 Feb 8 1728. Appraisers: John Abell, Samuel Abell. (Elizabeth's siblings)
> Creditors: John Hall, James Smith.
> Next of kin: "minors". Administratrix: Elisabeth Haddock.
> ===
> John Haddock 10.206 A SM £14.7.3 £28.1.10 Mar 4 1729
> Sureties: John Hall, William Hall.
> Received from: John Hall, William Hall, John Sweetman, Jonathon Seale, John Leatherland, Hugh Hopewell, Owen Mackan, John Mackentoss, Charles Ganiard.
> Payments to: James Smith, Jonathon Seale, John Hall.
> Administratrix: Elisabeth Pickering, wife of Jeremiah Pickering (also Jeremiah Pickering).
> (Research notes by Donna Cooper, 2003)

His son, John II was the administrator to his step-father's (Jeremiah) will in 1745. Jeremiah made a will in April of 1745 and died in May of 1745. He named John II Haddock as the executor of his will in 1745, so John was of age and was the oldest of the Haddock children. John's mother was about 52 when she re-married Jeremiah. Since Jeremiah did not name a child of his own and asked one of his wife's children to execute the will, it probable that he had no sons or no children. [Ref: Calendar of Wills, Vol. 9, 1744 -1749, Calendar of Wills 1744-1749] Pickrel, Jeremiah, St. Mary's Co., MD 28 April 1745. Probated 6 May 1745. To John Hadack, bequeath all belongings, heir to estate. Witness: Thomas Forrest, Francis Hutchins. [24.91] [Maryland Probates and Estates] Jeremiah Prickrel [1.289] Saint Mary's County, MD. [59.1.11] May 6, 1745, Aug 5, 1745 Appraisers: Samuel Abell, Acquilla Hutchens. Creditors: George Plater, Abraham Barnes. Administrator and Executor: John Haddock. It also mentioned Samuel Abell, John's maternal grandfather as an appraiser in the will.

How they got to Virginia/Maryland

The Chesapeake Bay area is thought to have been first explored by Europeans in the early 1500s. The English Captain John Smith later explored and mapped this region in the early 1600s. However, the colony of Maryland was not chartered until 1632 or formally settled until 1634. It was originally intended by its proprietors, George Calvert—the first Lord Baltimore—and his son Cecilius (Cecil)—the second Lord Baltimore—to be a refuge for English Catholics and a source of family prosperity.

Calvert's heir, the second Lord Baltimore, Cecil Calvert, organized the expedition to found the colony. To ensure political support for the charter in England, Cecil remained behind. His brother Leonard lead the expedition and served as the colony's first governor. In keeping with his father's wishes to promote religious toleration and help ensure the colony's financial success, Cecil invited both Catholics and Protestants to settle Maryland. Most of the settlers—about 140 in number—were Protestants (as best as can be gathered from the historical records). Many were indentured servants. The settlers also included about 20 gentlemen, some of their wives, and two Catholic priests.

On November 22, 1633, the settlers, aboard Cecil's two ships, the *Ark* and the *Dove,* left Cowes on the Isle of Wight, England, for the Maryland colony. They took a southern route, surviving stormy weather and even being separated from each other. Then they stopped for supplies in the West Indies before reaching Chesapeake Bay in early March 1634. On March 25, 1634, the settlers rowed ashore to a small island, which they named St. Clement's, located in the mouth of the Potomac River (part of the Chesapeake Bay water basin). They gave thanks and held what is the first Catholic Mass in the English colonies. Their thanksgiving is now celebrated as Maryland Day, a state holiday.

Summary of Maryland settlement

1633, Nov. 22. English settlers on *Ark* and *Dove* set sail from Cowes, England (on modern map, this would be the Isle of Wright), for Maryland. The journey is documented in a small publication listed below:

A Briefe Relation of the Voyage Unto Maryland, by Father Andrew White

1634, March 25. Landing of settlers at <u>St. Clement's Island</u> (now Blakistone Island) (<u>Maryland Day</u>). Calvert party celebrated Feast of Annunciation (March 25); later purchased Indian land, and built a "Fort at <u>St. Mary's City</u>."

" ... then on the 3 of March came into Chesapeake bay, at the mouth of Patomecke (Potamac), this baye is the most delightfull water I ever saw, between two sweet lande, with a channell, 4:5:6: 7: and 8 fathoms deepe, some 10 leagues broad...." (From Father Andrew White's *A Briefe Relation of the Voyage Vnto Maryland)*

The preface from this small publication:

Father Andrew White's *A Briefe Relation of the Voyage Vnto Maryland* is one of the most important first-hand accounts of the early European settlement of North America.

It is reprinted here from the Maryland Historical Society Fund Publication no. 35 (1899). Father White's original manuscript was given to Leonard Calvert, who was the brother of Lord Baltimore, leader of the expedition, and first governor of the province. Calvert sent it to Sir Richard Lechford, his business partner in England, in May 1634.

The Briefe Relation is of singular importance in the understanding of the voyage and first settlement of the Maryland colony in 1633 and 1634, and of the larger social and political context in which these events occurred.

By all accounts, Father White's career was as exciting as the time in which he lived. During his seventy-eight years, he was a priest of the order of the Society of Jesus, a scholar, a teacher, a missionary, a student of American Indian languages, and an advisor to the Lords Baltimore in shaping their plans to establish the Maryland colony. He suffered for his religious convictions. As a Catholic priest, he was twice arrested, imprisoned, and banished from his native England. When, at age fifty-five, he stepped ashore with Leonard Calvert and the first Maryland settlers at St. Clement's Island on March 25, 1634, he had already seen much of Europe. He survived repeated contests with fever in the New World to continue his missionary work among the English settlers and the Indian nations he found on the shores of the Chesapeake Bay and its tributaries. Note: Father White was also credited as converting the Chief of the Piscataway Indians and his daughter, Mary Kittamaquund in 1640-41. Mary was sent by her father to St. Mary's City to be educated.

Father White's *Briefe Relation* allows us the privilege of seeing the New World through the eyes of the "first adventurers." It enables us to walk in the footsteps of the 140 men and women who crossed a vast ocean aboard the *Ark* and the *Dove* to carve a settlement out of the wilderness and to build a new society founded on principles of freedom and opportunity (end of preface).

So, St. Mary's was on the mouth of the Potomac River which fed out from Washington, D.C.

1634-1694. St. Mary's City served as capital of Maryland.

1637. St. Mary's County first cited in provincial records.

1639. First elections in province for delegates to Assembly ordered by Governor Calvert on Kent Island, and in hundreds of Mattapanient, St. Michael's, St. Mary's, and St. George's.

1645, Feb. 14-1646, Dec. Ingle's Rebellion: Richard Ingle led rebellion against proprietary government.

1649, April 21. Religious toleration law (An Act concerning Religion) enacted.

1652, March 29. Parliamentary commissioners displaced proprietary regime.

1657. Lord Baltimore reestablished proprietary authority over Maryland.

1667. St. Mary's City incorporated.

1689, July-1690, May. Maryland Revolution of 1689. Protestant Associators overthrew proprietary officers.

1694/5, Feb. Capital moved from St. Mary's City to Anne Arundel Town.

1695. State House at St. Mary's City used for County Courthouse.

1698. Hospital established at Cool Springs, Charlotte Hall.

Remember, 1685 was when Benjamin and James migrated to Maryland. By the time, John I moved to Maryland and married, there was a well-established settlement already operating.

The first record of John Haddock in Maryland shows him obtaining the right to practice law, next was marrying Elizabeth Abell in 1716 when he was 63 years old (no other record of his marriage was found, even in England). If this is one in the same John Haddock from England, then he was old by standards of the day by the time he married and had children. However, most family tree research supports common acceptance of these records. Because this is an important link between ancestors of the old world and new world, I have spent extra time researching this ancestor and records of the area to make it more cohesive.

What we know about John I Haddock: In the records, it could have been that he was referred to as a 'papist of the parish,' which was a disparaging term used during this time meaning he was loyal to the Pope rather than the Church of England or the king. So, some of our ancestors were probably Catholic, even though it appears his cousin, James Haddock, was an Anglican priest. The Catholics figured in to the colonization of the new world due to converting the natives who lived in the region. In other records of the time, John Haddock of Sherwood St. was referred to as a 'victualler,' a guy who furnished victuals, or provisions to a ship or a person. If not the same John, this man was probably related since the job was enjoyed by other Haddock ancestors. Also, Richard had enjoyed the same title and was the first victualler for the entire English Navy.

Newspaper Reports

From old newspaper archives of the late 1600's to 1800's, we know that the states of Maryland and Virginia published news of the Americas along with Great Britain and the rest of Europe. The Virginia Gazette and the Federal Gazette regularly published activity of the British Navy, mentioning Admiral (Nicholas) Haddock's activities during 1738-1739 as a conflict grew between Spain and Great Britain. Events of 1720 added to an ongoing conflict with Spain when the collapse of the South Sea Company's shares caused financial crisis in London and ruined many investors, possibly even some of the Haddock family. The rapid inflation and the speculation mania it had encouraged become known as the South Sea Bubble. In short, this was a scheme to reduce national debt by transferring stock ownership of the company in lieu of citizens collecting debt owned by the government.

The colonies had special interest in this conflict because it would end up involving recruits to the British Army from the colonies for the first time. In addition, regular shipping news was reported that named ship Captains and occasionally there were some named Haddock. For example, the Captain Haddock of Rye, England who commanded the Stag, revenue cutter ship was reported to be transporting British soldiers in August, 1794. Another ship captain, Roger Haddock, was mentioned as operating in the area. They even had classified ads that reported indentured servants who absconded and were being hunted, including a man named Haddock from Ireland who had run away from his obligations. Therefore, people who lived near the cities did have access to the news and continued to have an interest in what was going on in the homeland. With the Haddocks having connections to relatives in the shipping industry, there's no doubt they could travel back and forth, if desired.

PART III

Pitt County, North Carolina

In North Carolina, we continue documented family history. Like the Richards in England, we have several Johns in North Carolina and it gets confusing keeping the lineage correct. Therefore, I continue numbering them: I, II, III. The 1790 Census listed John Haddock, Sr. as a planter in Pitt County, North Carolina, whom I have identified as John Haddock II, to make it easier to follow. He is the first of several ancestors listed as "planter," during this period which is another word they used for farmer. Over 1700 acres of land were recorded in his name in the office of the Register of Deeds. Until recently, no record was known of his date of birth, but it is estimated he was born around 1720. Now we know this is the same John II, who was born in Maryland and moved to North Carolina. He married Liscom(b) Hall TAYLOR and they had at least six children (see Appendix III).

Most early settlers in North Carolina earned a living by farming. They grew tobacco, wheat, and corn. Corn became a staple in colonial times. People ate corn on the cob, and made grits and cornbread from corn. They also fed corn to the animals.

In that same census, there was a total of 4 Haddocks listed as living in Pitt County, North Carolina: Admiral, William, Charles, and John. We are assuming they were brothers and some family researchers have tracked which direction they and their descendants migrated. This writer will follow the same paths.

Additionally, there were two families each of Bucks and Mills. These families intermarried with the Haddocks and even moved on with them, in some cases.

John I Haddock's son, John II Haddock was born about 1721 in St. Mary's Co., MD. So, we can estimate that John II moved to North Carolina sometime around 1740 because he married there in 1742 and, later, must have had to return to Maryland to help execute his stepfather's will. Most likely, he traveled the Carolina trail, which was part of the King's Highway. Alternatively, he traveled by water as he probably had connections to people in the shipping business. It could have been both water and by land, since the trip from Maryland to Virginia was just across the Potomac River.

How they got there

It is approximately 200 miles from St. Mary's County, Maryland to Pitt County, North Carolina. If the weather held positive, then a wagon could travel about 15 miles a day, making the trip last about 2 weeks. Here's a bit about how people migrated to the lower colonies:

The heavily traveled Great Wagon Road, part of what was called, the King's Highway, was the primary route for the early settlement of the Southern United States, particularly the "backcountry". Although a wide variety of settlers traveled southward on the road, two dominant cultures emerged. The German Palatines and Scotch-Irish American immigrants arrived in huge numbers because of unendurable conditions in Europe. The Germans (also known as Pennsylvania Dutch) tended to find rich farmland and work it zealously to become stable and prosperous. The other group (known also as Presbyterian or Ulster Scots) tended to be restless, clannish, and fiercely independent; they formed what became known as the Appalachian Culture. Partly because of the language difference, the two groups tended to keep to themselves.

Beginning at the port of Philadelphia, where many immigrants entered the colonies, the Great Wagon Road passed through the towns of Lancaster and York in southeastern Pennsylvania. Turning southwest, the road crossed the Potomac River and entered the Shenandoah Valley near present-day Martinsburg, West Virginia. It continued south in the valley via the Great Warriors' Trail, also called the Indian Road, which was established by centuries of Indian travel over ancient trails created by migrating buffalo herds. The Shenandoah portion of the road is also known as the Valley Pike. The Treaty of Lancaster in 1744 had established colonists' rights to settle along the Indian Road. Although traffic on the road increased dramatically after 1744, it was reduced to a trickle during the French and Indian War (Seven Years' War) from 1756 to 1763. But after the war ended, it became the most heavily traveled road in America.

What the historians say: NORTH CAROLINA

The French were the first known white people to explore the North Carolina coast. Spaniards also came to the region, but neither they nor the French established any permanent settlements.

In 1585, Sir Walter Raleigh of England sent an expedition to settle on Roanoke Island. This group became the first English colony in America. But misfortunes forced the settlers to return to England in 1586. Raleigh sent a later expedition to Roanoke Island in 1587, with John White as governor. White established a colony and sailed back to England for supplies that same year. When Queen Elizabeth allowed White to return to Roanoke Island in 1590, his colony had disappeared. No one knows what happened to the more than a hundred men, women, and children of what has come to be called the Lost Colony.

Remember, Maryland's first settlement was established in 1634, so efforts at settling North Carolina began before Maryland, as far as we know.

In 1629, King Charles I of England granted his attorney general, Sir Robert Heath, the southern part of the English claim in America. This included a strip of land containing what is now both North Carolina and South Carolina and extending to the Pacific Ocean. The land was named the "Province of Carolana" (land of Charles). Sir Heath made no attempts at a settlement.

The first permanent white settlers in Carolina came from Virginia. They settled in the Albemarle Sound region around 1650. In 1663, Charles II of England re-granted Carolina to eight of his favorite nobles. He made them "lords proprietors" (ruling landlords) of the colony. The proprietors divided Carolina into three counties: (1) Albermarle, in the northern region; (2) Clarendon, in the Cape Fear region; and (3) Craven, in what is now South Carolina. In 1664, William Drummond was appointed governor of Albermarle County and government began in Carolina. Clarendon County lasted only until 1667. From then until 1689, Albermarle County had the only government in the North Carolina region.

During the late 1600's and early 1700's, increasing numbers of settlers came to North Carolina. In 1705, North Carolina's first town, Bath, was incorporated near the mouth of the Pamlico River. By 1710, settlements had spread down the coast and along the riverbanks, as far south as the Neuse River. In 1710, Swiss and Germans founded New Bern, a community several miles inland on the Neuse, in Tuscarora Indian territory.

New Bern was one of the most peaceful and prosperous settlements in North Carolina, until dawn on September 22, 1711, at which time disaster struck. Enraged Tuscarora tribesmen, whose land had been seized by white settlers, attacked New Bern and other settlements. Within two hours, most of the settlements between the Neuse and Pamlico rivers lay in ruins. The Indians had massacred hundreds of settlers, burned their homes, stolen their valuables and destroyed their crops. The massacre marked the beginning of the Tuscarora War, the worst Indian war in North Carolina's history. The colonists defeated the Indians on March 25, 1713. (Note: About 35,000 Indians, belonging to about 30 tribes, lived in the North Carolina region when white people first arrived. The most important tribes were the Cherokee in the western mountains; the Hatteras along the coast; and the Catawba, Chowanoc, and Tuscarora of the coastal plain and the Piedmont.)

While settlers battled the wilderness and the Indians during the late 1600's and early 1700's, pirates terrorized North Carolina's coastline. Remember, piracy was encouraged by the aristocracy in England, partly to encourage building up the navy and partly for personal profit. Most piracy along the Atlantic Coast ended with the death of the famous pirate Blackbeard in a battle near Ocracoke Island in 1718.

In 1729, the lords' proprietors sold their land back to England. North Carolina became a royal colony, ruled by royal governors appointed by the king. These governors ruled wisely and well, and helped the colony grow. In 1729, only about 36,000 persons lived in North Carolina, mostly along the coast where the richest soil was. By 1775, the population had grown to nearly 350,000 and settlement had spread westward across the Piedmont and into the mountains. Remember, our ancestor, John II, moved to North Carolina, between 1740-1742, during this time of rapid growth.

The key event that affected North Carolina's development until the time of the Revolution was King George II's takeover of North Carolina from the heirs of the Lords Proprietors in 1729. The change generated a land bonanza in the colony as the Crown eased land purchase requirements and sent out the equivalent of real estate agents to drum up business. Their work, and the encouragement of royal governors, touched off a boom in North Carolina that lasted from 1730 to the American Revolution. (Goldfield, 2005)

Beginnings of long documented family history in the U S

When John II was born, Freemasonry was in it's infancy. Freemasonry is the world's oldest and largest fraternity. It has existed in its current form since 1717 and men of good character throughout the past 300 years have been attracted to it. Freemasonry does not solicit membership, so our relatives formed a positive opinion of the organization and petitioned for membership. He (the candidate, male only membership) was investigated as to his morals and character and found at the time of his petition to be living a life consistent with the high purposes and aims of the organization. Hopefully he maintained that standard throughout the balance of his life. So, when the information is available, membership in the Masons will be noted along with religious preference.

Focus: John II G Haddock (1720-1809)

Birth

JOHN II G HADDOCK was the oldest child, born in 1720 in St Mary's City, Maryland to Elizabeth Abell, age 43, and **JOHN I** Haddock, age 67.

At age 5, JOHN II G's younger brother, William A, was born in 1725 in St Mary's County, Maryland when JOHN G was 5 years old. Some records show William's middle name as Admiral. William A Haddock - 1725–1764 – died at 39 and buried in Rowan County, North Carolina, a predominately Presbyterian community populated mostly with Scots-Irish people. He and his wife died the same year during a time of economic depression following a 10-year drought while a regulation war was building in the county. William A also moved from Maryland to North Carolina during his life. If one traces where his children are reported born, then we can estimate that William moved around 1750, some 8 years after his brother.

Occupation

Planter/farmer/plantation owner.

Marriage

John II was about 22 when married Liscom Hall TAYLOR in 1742 in Pitt County, North Carolina, so he would have already moved there by this time.

I noticed that Liscom's middle name was Hall and thought it could be a family name, but could not find a direct connection to the Hall family that were named in the settlement of John I's estate. John I obviously did business with the Hall family and, later, the Hall (Haul) name showed up as middle names in other Haddock descendants. As usual in those days, they probably lived on adjoining land and, possibly, moved together as families. This is another project for further research.

When John II moved away from Maryland, he left the area (New England) where education was most emphasized and supported. As he and other ancestors moved into virgin country, their energy was spent mostly on surviving, establishing a home, clearing land and growing food. In families, the fathers were more educated and probably spent time with the kids mostly on religious education. Consequently, there may have been a decline in basic education for pioneers who ventured out moving into unsettled territories.

John II and Liscomb had about 10 children (8 sons) in 23 years. He died on September 29, 1809, in Chicod, North Carolina, having lived a long life of 89 years, and was buried there.

Residence(s)

JOHN G HADDOCK lived in Beaufort County, North Carolina, in 1755. Beaufort County was broken into smaller sections and became Pitt County in 1760.

JOHN G HADDOCK lived in Pitt County, North Carolina, in 1762. (Source: 1762, Early Tax List, Pitt County, NC)

JOHN G HADDOCK lived in Pitt County, North Carolina, in 1764. (Source: 1764, No Township Listed, Pitt County, NC)

JOHN G HADDOCK lived in Pitt County, North Carolina, in 1790.

JOHN II G HADDOCK lived in Greenville, North Carolina, in 1800.

Birth of Children

His first son, Andrew was born in 1742 in Chicod, North Carolina. Since there were other Andrews, he is designated as a Sr to distinguish him from his descendants. Andrew Haddock Sr. - 1742–1793. He died in North Carolina.

Next, another son, whom I have designated as **John III**, was born in 1744 in Pitt County, North Carolina. JOHN G Haddock III - 1744–1821. Died in Georgia.

John II's 3rd son, William A, was born in 1749 in Pitt County, North Carolina: William A Haddock - 1749–1821. Died in North Carolina.

His 4th son, Zachariah, was born in 1751 in Pitt County, North Carolina: Zachariah Haddock - 1751–1826. Murdered in Florida.

His 5th son, Admiral (b 1753), was born in 1753 in Pitt County, North Carolina: Admiral Haddock - 1753–1820. Died in South Carolina.

His son Charles was born in 1755 in Pitt County, North Carolina. Charles Haddock - 1755–1820. Died in Georgia.

His son Richard W was born in 1757 in Pitt County, North Carolina. Richard W Haddock - 1757–1830. Died in North Carolina.

His son Peter was born in 1764 in Pitt County, North Carolina. Peter Haddock - 1764–1820. Died in Georgia.

His daughter Nancy was born in 1764 in Chicod, North Carolina. Nancy Haddock - 1764–1826

His daughter Liscom was born in 1765 in Chicod, North Carolina. Liscom Haddock - 1765–1845

Mentioned in Will

In 1745, John II was mentioned in his step-father's (Pickering) will in St Mary's County, Maryland, USA, which may have required a trip back to Maryland.

Land Transaction

Given below is one of the earliest deeds for John Haddock- taken from the text of Haddock Heritage, Second Edition, pub 2003, by Donna Haddock Cooper. In 1757, a deed was located in North Carolina in Beaufort Co., NC, and, in abstract.

The Scots-Irish Immigrants in the Carolinas

In 1764, JOHN G. HADDOCK II was living in North Carolina during the arrival and settlement of Scots-Irish immigrants in the Carolinas. Later, we find the Burns family of Scots-Irish living in the Branom community, Hopkins County, Texas and intermarrying with the Haddock ancestors. One Reverend Laird Burns, who is buried in Mt Zion Cemetery, Hopkins County, lived in the Carolinas during the late 1700's.

Death of Brother

JOHN G's brother William died in 1764 in Rowan County, North Carolina when JOHN G was 44 years old. Rowan County is about 200 miles west of Pitt County, which means William moved further west, closer to South Carolina, before he died.

William A Haddock - 1725–1764

The Stamp Act

The Stamp Act was passed by the British Parliament on March 22, 1765. The new tax was imposed on all American colonists and required them to pay a tax on every piece of printed paper they used. Ship's papers, legal documents, licenses, newspapers, other publications, and even playing cards were taxed. The money collected by the Stamp Act was to be used to help pay the costs of defending and protecting the American frontier near the Appalachian Mountains (10,000 troops were to be stationed on the American frontier for this purpose). (https://www.history.org/history/teaching/tchcrsta.cfm, n.d.)

When people took to the streets to protest the Stamp Act in 1765, JOHN G. HADDOCK II was probably living in North Carolina, one of the colonies opposing British rule.

Death of Son

His son Andrew passed away on May 15, 1793, at the age of 51._Andrew Haddock Sr. - 1742–1793

Death of Wife

His wife Liscom Hall passed away on December 26, 1802, in Chicod, North Carolina, at the age of 81. They had been married 60 years.

Death

JOHN II G HADDOCK died on September 29, 1809, in Chicod, North Carolina, when he was 89 years old.

Cemetery notes and/or description: This is a family burial plot located on the old Haddock Plantation property at Chicod, Pitt County, North Carolina, USA. It is also known as the Mack Smith Family Cemetery, Adams Graveyard, and Adams-Smith Cemetery.

They must have been failing in health because he made deeds in May of 1802 disposing of almost a thousand acres of land, but reserving some of the land for himself and Liscom to use until their death. He was then about 82 years of age. Liscom witnessed these deeds.

John II was still living as late as February 11, 1806, when he was a party to a deed of some land in which both he and John, III. (or Jr.), had an interest. The land was sold to John William, grandson of John II, who paid 300 pounds to his grandfather for his grandfather's interest in the property. John, III, the father, did not receive money from his son for his share, but did receive the use of the land for himself and his wife "Rody," as long as they pleased throughout their lifetime. Again, there is much confusion over who was Sr. and who as Jr. with use of the name John in the Haddock family.

Summary of John II's life:

We estimate that John II moved to North Carolina in his early 20's and married there where he had his family and lived until his death. (See Appendix III)

As mentioned, the 1790 census found four brothers, John III, (there was also a John, Sr, whom I designated John II) Charles, William, and Admiral married and living in Pitt County, North Carolina. A sister, Nancy Haddock Richards also lived in the area. These would most likely be John II's children. Pitt County reportedly has a place called "Haddock's Crossroads" near Winterville, just south of Greensboro (Greenville). Records show Nancy died in Boone County, Missouri.

John II's 4th son, Zachariah was not found still living in the area by 1790, but married in 1785 while still living in North Carolina. Legends say he went to Florida, then returned north into Georgia, perhaps Camden County, just north of the Florida boundary. Records do show he was buried in Florida. The most current research show Zachariah was murdered in Florida by the husband of a woman with whom he and his son were traveling. This is another story that need further investigation by someone who wants to research the details.

There has been much speculation and confusion on the name Admiral. Since the Haddocks who remained in England were seafaring people, it was only natural that they would be attracted to service in the fleet when the King increased the number of ships on the high seas. Several of them served in distinguished positions. As mentioned in the first section, Richard Haddock was knighted and became Sir Richard Haddock. He served as Admiral and Comptroller of the English Navy. His son, Nicholas Haddock, also became an Admiral in the English Navy. Nicholas was still serving in the English Navy as late as 1742 and died in 1746.

To add to the confusion, John I seems to have named his 2nd son, William with the middle name of Admiral. I suggest that John II named his 5th son, Admiral (b. abt 1753), because of pride in knowing at least two Haddocks had achieved the rank of Admiral in the Navy, similar to the present practice of naming children after famous men and women. The younger Admiral (b. 1774) was probably named for his uncle, John II's brother. The different Admirals will be distinguished by their year of birth. William A is just referred to as 'William A.'

The confusion carries on to the wife of either Admiral (older or younger). Different sources will show both was married to Selah "Celia" Nelson. The dates seem to match best on the older Admiral's wife. Legend says she was a descendant of the famous Nelson family of England but it is not documented. Reportedly, her people settled first in Virginia, then moved to North Carolina. They were large people, many of them being over six feet tall and were talented blacksmiths. Her father was Lott Nelson and her grandfather, James Nelson. She had a brother, Nimrod. There seems to be no documented connection to the Nelson family in England and, if so, the connection would be through Nelson's illegitimate daughter, Horatia. There are stories surrounding one of each Admiral's descendants that will be told later in this work. It looks like they both ended up living in the state of Georgia. Stay tuned!

The Revolutionary War

Reportedly, at least two Haddocks from North Carolina served in the Revolutionary War, but it is unclear if they were directly related. An elder Admiral (probably b. 1753) was a private for 30 months and was granted 228 acres of land. A John Haddock (probably John II) is listed as serving, but no record was found that he received land. This would be a good project for an ancestor who wants to verify these hints. I have found that if a researcher discovers an ancestor who has membership with the DAR (daughters of the American republic) there probably would be a proof of lineage that can be obtained for the asking. It may be obvious that I have not looked very closely into the service record of our descendants during this time in history. This makes for another research project.

As early as 1764, John Haddock, III, son of John, II, was granted land along Swift Creek by King George III. The tract contained 100 acres. Approximately two years later, John III Haddock married Rhoda Taylor, daughter of William and Dinah Taylor. Her grandfather was also William Taylor.

William Taylor, Jr., deeded 200 acres of land to John Haddock, III on January 22, 1767. This may have been a dowry for his daughter, Rhoda. John promptly sold it the next day for 120 pounds. Since the father-in-law signed as a witness, he was probably agreeable to the sale. Proof the two men were on good terms was shown on April 24, 1791, when William Taylor, Jr., deeded a slave to his son-in-law "with love and affection." On April 4, 1793, he deeded household items and a Negro to John "with love and affection." This last deed was witnessed by Nancy Haddock (Nancy Haddock Richards), who was the sister of John, III.

John III was married to Liscom (born TAYLOR) and his marriage is often confused with his son's (John William) marriage to Rhoda Catherine Taylor. They were related: John William, John III's son married Rhoda, William Taylor, Jr's daughter. That would make Liscom the aunt of Rhoda. Children born to John William and Rhoda with the approximate year of their birth were John, 1770; Nancy, 1772; Admiral, b.1774; Zachariah, 1779; and Charles, 1780. There was also a daughter, Elizabeth, and perhaps other children (see Appendix V) Thanks to my sister, Maredia Haddock Cunningham for helping clear up this confusion.

After the Revolutionary War, free land, offered by newly-opened territories in western Georgia, Alabama, northern Florida, and even as far into the frontier as Mississippi and Indiana, drained some parts of North Carolina and caused considerable hardship on those choosing to stay. Between 1815 and 1850, more than one-third (1/3) of the state's population emigrated westward - primarily due to a struggling economy, indifference to education, resistance to taxation for any reason, and general backwardness.

Because John III is a pivotal ancestor in keeping the lineage straight, we pause briefly to focus on him and his family in more depth.

Focus: John III G Haddock (1744-1821)

When John III G Haddock was born in 1744 in Pitt County, North Carolina, his father, John II, was 24 and his mother, Liscom, was 23. John III married Rhoda Catherine TAYLOR on May 4, 1766, in North Carolina. They had several children in 23 years. He moved from North Carolina to Georgia and died in 1821 in Jones County, near Macon, Georgia, having lived a long life of 77 years, and was buried in Haddock, Georgia. His brother, Admiral (b. 1753), also moved to Georgia and, together, they established a long line of Haddocks who lived in and around Haddock, Jones County, Georgia.

Occupation

Constable. Homesteader/land speculator/pioneer and plantation owner.

Marriage

It was in North Carolina that John III G Haddock married Rhoda Catherine TAYLOR (1741–1809), apparently a niece of his mother, in 1766, when he was 23 years old.

Residence

John III G Haddock lived in Pitt County, North Carolina, until sometime after 1800 and by the 1820's had moved to Georgia.

Birth of Children

His son **John William** was born in 1767 in Pitt County, North Carolina. It appears John William stayed in North Carolina when his parents moved to Georgia. Note that John William had already bought land in North Carolina from his grandfather John II.

John III's daughter Elizabeth was born in 1769 in Chicod, North Carolina and died there.

His daughter Nancy Haddock was born in 1772 in Pitt County, North Carolina and passed away in Kentucky at the age of 48. Nancy Haddock Whichard - 1772–1820.

His son Admiral (b. 1774) was born in Chicod, North Carolina, but later moved to Jones County, Georgia. Admiral Haddock - 1774–1860.

His daughter Esther was born on May 12, 1780, in Pitt County, North Carolina. Esther Haddock - 1780–1870. Died in Kentucky.

His son Charles was born in 1780 in Chicod, North Carolina. Charles Haddock - 1780–1859. Died in Kansas after living in Missouri. There are several Charles' in the family, so each is distinguished by birth dates.

His son Henry was born in 1790 in Pitt County, North Carolina and passed away in 1799 in Chicod, North Carolina, at the age of 9. Henry Haddock - 1790–1799.

Georgia Land Lotteries

John G. Haddock III lived in Georgia in 1821, a time when the state redistributed about 75 percent of its land, mostly belonging to the native Americans. This was probably a major incentive for his move to Georgia.

Death

John III G Haddock died in 1821 in Jones County, Georgia, when he was 78 years old and is reportedly buried in the Haddock cemetery there near Haddock, Jones County, Georgia, United States.

Summary of John III's life:

It appears that John, III, became a man of substantial means. He owned considerable acreage of land and slaves, both in North Carolina and in Georgia. He was highly respected in the community and served as Constable, an office that held the prestige and responsibilities more like a sheriff than that of present-day constables. Looking at his history of buying and selling land, then moving on to obtain more land, I would say that he was quite the business man.

The children in this family moved west to Kentucky, Kansas, and ultimately, Missouri, south to Georgia, and some remained in North Carolina. Each move in each direction seemed to be about 200 miles, which translated into roughly a 2-week trip. Maybe this was considered a reasonable length of time to expect a family to be on the move. For a single person to travel back and forth on horseback, averaged about 40 miles a day, thus about a 5 days' journey. (See Appendix IV)

Brief Detour: Spotlight on Alonzo L Haddock

A Georgia descendent of the older Admiral (b.1753), Alonzo L reportedly shot and killed a man near the turn of the century in Haddock, Georgia. The story and resulting trial made the news all the way to Atlanta. It seems the murder centered around one of the orphaned daughters in the extended Haddock family who had attracted the attention of an older man. This led to conflict and warnings. When they encountered each other one morning, the other guy lay dead. The trial found Alonzo not guilty of murder due to the extenuating circumstances. This is yet, another research project for a serious family researcher, as it makes for a good story and there was a lot reported in the news at the time around 1908 or so.

What the historians say: Slavery

Slavery, the practice in which people own other people, probably followed the development of planting and farming, which was a labor-intensive operation. The enslavement of blacks in the American Colonies began during the 1600's.

Most slaves, in what became the Southern States, worked on plantations that grew chiefly indigo, rice, sugar or tobacco.

Field hands worked longer than any other kind of slave. Their workday generally lasted from sunrise to sunset. Some field hands were housed as well as free workers, but many others lived under the worst conditions (The World Book Encyclopedia, 1979c).

Haddocks owned slaves, as was the customs of that time and place. The conflict of opinions between the northern states and southern states eventually resulted in the American Civil War. Haddocks were also involved in this struggle and fought on both sides, especially for the confederacy where most lived.

More Family History

By 1800, the younger generation had begun to marry and establish homes. **John William**, the son of John, III, married Nancy MILLS about 1786 and listed at least two children, one daughter, Liscom who was buried in Georgia. Her brother, **Nasby Hall Haddock**, is our direct descendant. While **John III** moved to Georgia and died there along with his wife and daughter, **John William** stayed in North

Carolina as did **Nasby Hall Haddock**. It appears that the Haddock and Mills families lived close together and intermarried. There are Haddocks and Mills families buried in the Mt Zion Cemetery, Hopkins County, Texas, but no proof the Mills are related. This is yet, another research project for the family researcher.

Charles, John William's brother, stayed a while in North Carolina, and was married after 1800. His first wife, reportedly, was a Cherokee Indian maiden named Wallraven. It appears he married again in 1804 to Penelope Penny Mills, another one of the Mills family, and eventually lived in Missouri and died in Kansas.

Zachariah married Cloe (or Cloey) Albritton about 1803. Her mother's given name was Unice. By 1810, Zachariah's fourth child was born. Zachariah also ended up in Missouri and was buried there.

Zachariah and Charles were only a year apart in age. They developed a closeness that was to last throughout their lives. Charles was the bold one, always ready to strike out for new adventure, while Zachariah was of a quiet and studious nature. He made a good balance wheel for the pair.

It was reported that Zachariah was a beautiful penman and his spelling was outstanding for those days. The lives of the two brothers were so intertwined that in later generations we found one never spoke of Charles or Zachariah alone, it was always "Charles and Zachariah" or "Zachariah and Charles" (Haddock & Haddock, undated).

Focus: John William Haddock (1767-1822)

The next ancestor in our lineage, as mentioned, is **John W**. When JOHN W Haddock was born in 1767 in Chicod, North Carolina, his father, JOHN III, was 23 and his mother, Rhoda, was 24. John W married Nancy MILLS in 1786 in Pitt County, North Carolina. This would be one of two generations of Haddocks who married (sisters) into the Mills family. These families both lived in Pitt County and must have had property that joined each other. John W and Nancy had two children (that we know about) during their marriage, all born in North Carolina. He died in 1822 in his hometown, at the age of 55, and was buried there.

JOHN W. Haddock lived in Chicod, North Carolina in 1767 as American colonists created the foundation of a burgeoning new country.

Occupation

Plantation owner/planter

61

Marriage

As stated, JOHN W Haddock married Nancy MILLS (1768–1830) in 1786 in Pitt County, North Carolina, when he was 19 years old.

Residence

JOHN W Haddock lived in Greenville, North Carolina, in 1800 and still lived there in 1810.

Birth of Children

His daughter Liscom was born in 1765 in Chicod, North Carolina. Liscom Haddock - 1765–1845

 His son Nasby Hall was born in 1786. **Nasby Hall Haddock** - 1786–1859

Death

JOHN W Haddock died in 1822 in Chicod, North Carolina, when he was 55 years old and he was buried there. (See Appendix V)

Focus: Nasby Hall Haddock (1786-1859)

When Nasby Hall Haddock was born in 1786 his father, JOHN W, was 19 and his mother, Nancy, was 18. He married Sarah MILLS (his mother's younger sister) in 1804 in Pitt County, North Carolina. They had nine children in 27 years, one of whom was our next direct descendant, **Jordan David Haddock**. Their children were all born in North Carolina. Nasby Hall (probably went by 'Hall') died in June 1859 in Trenton, North Carolina, at the age of 73, and was buried there.

Occupation

Planter/plantation owner (owned up to 5 slaves, which meant he probably didn't try to farm large land holdings).

Marriage

As stated, Nasby Hall Haddock married Sarah Mills (1788–1845), in 1804 in Pitt County, North Carolina, when he was 18 years old.

Residence

Nasby Hall Haddock lived in Pitt County, North Carolina, in 1840 and lived there until he died.

Birth of Children

His son, our direct descendant, **Jordan David** was born in 1805 in Chicod, North Carolina. Jordan David Haddock - 1805–1861

His daughter Alice was born in 1808 in Pitt County, North Carolina. Alice Haddock - 1808–

His son Naseby was born in 1810. Naseby Haddock - 1810–

His son Nathen Spencer was born in 1818. Nathen Spencer Haddock - 1818–1867

His son Burton Hall was born in 1823 in Pitt County, North Carolina. Burton Hall Haddock - 1823–1880

His son William Haul was born in 1824 in North Carolina. William Haul Haddock - 1824–1868

His daughter Ms. Haddock F was born in 1825. Haddock F - 1825–

His son Joseph A was born in 1826 in Pitt County, North Carolina. Joseph A Haddock -1826–1875

The Panic of 1837

Banks shuttered their doors and unemployment skyrocketed when Nasby Hall Haddock lived in North Carolina in 1840, during the economic depression that became known as the Panic of 1837. This financial crisis in the United States touched off a major recession that lasted until the mid-1840s. Profits, prices, and wages went down while unemployment went up. Pessimism abounded during the time. (https://en.wikipedia.org/wiki/Panic_of_1837, n.d.)

Death of Wife

His wife Sarah passed away on December 26, 1845, in Camden County, Georgia, at the age of 57. They had been married 41 years. Note that other members of the family had already moved to Georgia and lived in this area. She may have been visiting there when she died.

Death

Nasby Hall Haddock died in June 1859 in Trenton, North Carolina, when he was 73 years old and was buried in the Haddock Family Cemetery. (See Appendix VI)

In summary, we find the Haddock family of documented history living in the North Carolina area during the late 1700s and early 1800s. At least two generations stayed on in North Carolina. They apparently prospered during this period, as evidenced by the land and other property which was mentioned in wills and deed transactions. These Haddocks had apparently settled in the planting and farming trade and raised rather large families, which was the custom of those days. By the late 1800's, some family members had already begun migrating to other states, such as Georgia, Florida, Missouri, and maybe Kentucky. Little else is known about their personalities and temperament, except that which has already been mentioned.

PART IV

Family Migration

Between 1807 and 1810 the close alliance of the Haddocks in Pitt County, North Carolina began breaking up. It should be noted that this coincides with the estimated time of death of John, III. In addition, land was becoming expensive and new land could be filed on at no cost in the west and south, which may have provided an additional incentive for the breakup.

Migration: Georgia

John Haddock, III, with his son, Admiral (1774), decided to go south. They sold their holdings and went to a vicinity south of Charleston, in Collecton County, the low country region of South Carolina, for a short time, then moved to a point near what is now Haddock, Georgia in Jones County. This was during the time of the Georgia Land Lotteries of 1821. It was in South Carolina that we see the last name Haddock take on different spellings. For example, some land transactions for Sara or Celia Nelson Haddock, apparently, Admiral's (1774) widow, was spelled 'Haddocks' on her will. Later, the name showed up on documents spelled, 'Haddox' and 'Hattox', both spelled more like it sounded as spelled on the will. I'm not sure if there were other reasons for allowing the change of spelling, such as avoiding financial or legal responsibilities. However, one group of Haddock ancestors in Georgia switched over to the alternate spelling.

There, an Admiral (1774) "Hadduck" filed claim on Cherokee land in Jones County, Georgia and a John Haddock filed 2 claims in Pulaski County. I think this is John III. (source: http://www.usgwarchives.net/ga/gafiles.htm) Older Haddock family members from Barry County, Missouri, recount stories of how John, III made this great move when he was "in his late sixties." A ripe age indeed, for a man to pull up roots and face new conditions. There are extensive documents listing the Haddocks who ended up in Georgia. A family history for this group is available. (Haddock H. R., 1976)

Migration: Kentucky & Missouri

Legends handed down in our family tell us that the two brothers, Charles and Zachariah, along with their aunt, Nancy (Haddock) Richards and her family, heard of the wonderful opportunities in Kentucky and decided to move west. They disposed of their property, prepared wagons and supplies, and sometime about 1810 or 1811 joined with settlers going west. Their trail wound upward through the Cumberland Gap and across Tennessee into Kentucky.

Soon another move came for the group. Charles, Nancy and their families joined with others going farther west. This time Zachariah and Cloey hesitated. Their children were growing up and the older ones had no desire to go farther. Also, Cloey could have been pregnant when the rest of the family moved. Either way, for the first time in their lives, Zachariah and Charles faced separation. Charles, with his penchant for adventure, could not bear to stay while Zachariah, with his consideration for his family, could not bring himself to go against their wishes. He reluctantly remained in Kentucky until after the birth of his son in 1815 and was listed there in the 1820 census. A daughter was born in Tennessee in 1826 proving they lived in Tennessee a while.

Family legends say the move west by Charles Haddock and Nancy (Haddock) Richards with their families was in a group led by Daniel Boon (or Boone), but the party may have used a trail scouted out by Boone. In any event, they settled in Boone County, Missouri.

Shortly after Charles Haddock, Jr., and Sarah Collins were married, they decided to join a small group moving to the Ozark region of Missouri near the northern border of Arkansas. It is believed that the families of Greenberry Easley and Joseph Hickam were in this group or followed soon after.

Preparations were made and one bright summer day in the early eighteen thirties they came poling up White River, probably in a keelboat, into what is now Barry County, Missouri on a long, narrow raft large enough to hold themselves, their stock and their scanty household possessions. A small stream, running into White River near where they finally settled, still bears the name Haddock Creek (Haddock & Haddock, undated).

The Ozark Mountain region was once called a "Lazy Man's Paradise". Food could be had in abundance just for the gathering. Deer, wild hogs, fox, raccoon, o'possum, skunk, squirrels and rabbits provided both meat and skins for tanning. Game birds such as geese, ducks, prairie chickens and quail were so thick that years later, after the railroad was built, these birds were shipped out by the carload. Rabbits were shipped out in large quantities up to the nineteen twenties. Wolves still populated the area during these days, but were not really in competition with humans for food because it was so abundant.

There were many varieties of fish in the rivers and creeks and the Haddocks, with their fisherman heritage, gloried in pulling them from the streams. It has been said in Barry County that a Haddock could catch a fish "any way it could be caught."

Papaws, grapes and wild blackberries, raspberries, gooseberries and huckleberries were prolific in season. Black walnuts, hickory nuts, hazel nuts and chinquapins were easily picked up and stored for winter. Honey was available to those with eyesight keen enough to trail a bee to the tree in which he had his hive. Perhaps best of all were the clear, sparkling springs that flowed forth in profusion from bluffs and hillsides, a source of pure drinking water. Anyone energetic enough to gather the bounty provided by nature need never go hungry.

Medicinal plants of many kinds were also plentiful. There was once a ginseng garden at the home of Milo B. Russell, the very garden where he and his wife, "Nicy," are now buried in Roaring River State Park in southern Missouri, near the northern border of Arkansas ("Nicy" was Unice, daughter of Zachariah Haddock).

Zachariah Haddock eventually came from Tennessee to Barry County, Missouri and is listed in the 1840 census of Barry County. However, on July 2, 1842, Zachariah died in Barry County leaving three children at home. Two of them married and established their own homes, but Lewis married and remained on the home place with his mother. Lewis died November 23, 1854. When his wife remarried, Cloey went to live with her daughter Unice (Mrs. Milo B. Russell), near the head of Roaring River. She was listed in the Russell home in the 1870 census, when she would have been 86 years old per her birthdate in the family Bible.

It is believed that Zachariah and Lewis Haddock were both buried in the Haddock cemetery near Eagle Rock, Missouri. This cemetery is so badly grown up, it is impossible to know how many are buried there. Most of the graves have flat limestone rocks chosen from the fields for head stones. Any names that were scratched into them have long since been obliterated.

When Cloey died, she was buried beside her daughter, Unice (Nicy), in the garden at the Russell home. Descendants, who visited the area when they were small, report seeing her gravestone many times. There were three adult graves and the grave of a small child in the plot. Over the years, stock was allowed in the garden and the stones were broken down. By the time the graves were fenced by the Roaring River Park Service, only the graves of Milo B. and "Nicy" Russell were identifiable.

Five children of Zachariah and Cloey married in Barry County, Missouri, between 1841 and 1846. They were Unice, Greenberry, Nancy, Lewis, and Mary. Penelope, the daughter of Charles Haddock, Sr., married Joel Petty in Barry County in 1841. A family history is available for this line. (Haddock H. R., undated)

Migration: Arkansas

Just south of Missouri we find another group of Haddock's settling in the Batesville, Arkansas area. It is assumed that **Jordan**, son of **Nasby Hall Haddock**, moved to Batesville after the birth of a daughter in 1848. Jordan Haddock is listed in the 1850 Census in St. Francis County, Arkansas. Living near them were the Buck, Corbit and Nesbit families. The Buck family lived in Pitt County, North Carolina and probably knew the Haddock family well. Like many Haddock relatives during this period, Jordan was a farmer. He married Sarah "Clemmy" Buck and they had ten children, of whom **Calvin** was the seventh. Rumored to be a rich man, Jordan deeded the land to the Liberty Church and cemetery in the skillet neighborhood just outside of Batesville. Jordan died on March 18, 1861 and was reportedly buried in Independence County, Arkansas, although his actual gravesite has not been identified. We track this line all the way to Texas to get to our current generation of Haddocks. The rest of this family history focuses on this line (**Calvin Cash Haddock**) of Haddocks.

North Carolina was the third most populous state in the Union in 1790, but by 1860 it had dropped to twelfth in population. Hundreds of thousands of White North Carolinians fled the state during those years, seeking cheap, fertile land in Tennessee, western Georgia, Indiana, Alabama, Missouri, Mississippi, and other trans-Allegheny states and territories. Thirty percent of North Carolina's native-born population, amounting to more than four hundred thousand persons, was living outside of the state in 1860.

How they got there

In 1834 a Raleigh newspaper reported that "our roads are thronged with emigrants to a more favored Country." As late as 1845, a Greensboro newspaper proclaimed, "On last Tuesday morning nineteen carts, with about one hundred persons, passed this place, from Wake County, on their way to the West."

An English visitor, wrote "these caravans consist of two or three covered wagons, full of women and children, furniture, and other necessaries, each drawn by a team of horses; brood mares, with foals by their sides, following; half a dozen or more cows, flanked on each side by the men, with their long rifles on their shoulders; sometimes a boy or two, or a half-grown girl on horseback."

Traveling by wagon trains, each group probably had a wagon master, someone who knew the trail. They even had rules. Here is an example for those days:

RULES OF THE WAGON TRAIN (GENERAL)

1. Allow 5 days for each one hundred miles. Bad days, what you can make, or stay in camp if agreed on by all. Real good days, and ground, makes it easy pulling 25 to 30 miles per day, if camp sites come right.

2. Take plenty of guns and ammunition.

3. Recommended - shave your head - Indians have no interest in bald heads.

4. Do not drink whisky or alcohol in freezing weather, or you are liable to freeze to death.

5. Do not fire rifles, only when absolutely necessary.

6. Do not stay up late - get your sleep. Guards are on duty all night.

7. Do not smoke strong pipes and cigars in close places where women and children are.

8. Keep your politics and preaching to yourself. Let the preacher do the preaching.

9. In case of a runaway of teams to wagons, get down and try to ride it out. If you jump, you are liable to get killed, or hurt badly. The horse men will pick the team up, maybe not too far off.

10. All people - young, married, or not, stay inside the circle of wagons in Indian country, or you are liable to lose your scalps.

11. The wagon master will try to pick spots so men and women and children can bathe, clean up, and wash clothes, when possible.

12. Be courteous and help others.

13. Do not be noisy, even with your musical instruments; only when it is safe.

14. When (we) can, we will have recreation and dances.

15. Do your part by all means. Church services will be held when it is considered safe from Indians, and other hazardous conditions. (Weir, 1909)

Reportedly, these rules could be renegotiated along the way, but the majority ruled.

Most often people moved because of free and/or low cost lands offered by the states. Consequently, they moved to lands like those they left in the East. Single families or family groups moved from mountainous areas in Appalachia, like North Carolina, to the Ozark Mountains or Ouachita Mountains and developed small farms and livestock operations.

They probably followed the Southwest Trail, which is a general term referring to a network of routes connecting the mid-Mississippi River Valley to the Red River valley (northeast Texas) in the 19th century. Most of the trail crossed Arkansas from the northeast to southwest. The trail avoided the swamps, which covered much of eastern Arkansas, while skirting the foothills of the Ozarks and the Ouachitas. This trail was also referred to as the Arkansas road, Red River road, Military Road. Native Americans likely used the trail long before the Louisiana Purchase in 1803. Others, especially early settlers, followed the rivers in keelboats. For example, the Yates family probably moved from Salt River, Adair, Missouri, which is due north of Miller County, Arkansas. They could have gone down the Mississippi River, then floated over and up the Red River, then spreading north and south on land from the Kiamichi River near what is now Paris, Texas.

What the historians say: Arkansas

In 1541, Hernando de Soto, a Spanish explorer, became the first European to reach the Mississippi River. He came upon it near what is now Memphis, Tennessee. De Soto crossed the Arkansas region to the Ozark Mountains. La Salle, the Frenchman, explored the area which he called Louisiana and claimed it for France in 1682. Another Frenchman built a camp at the mouth of the Arkansas River in 1686. Arkansas Post, the region's first permanent white settlement, developed near there.

In 1717, France chartered Louisiana to a firm called the Western Company. The company attempted to develop the resources of the Mississippi Valley. This venture brought several hundred colonists to the Arkansas region. But the venture failed, and many colonists left.

In 1763, after a series of wars in America, Spain received the land west of the Mississippi River. This land included the Louisiana Territory. In 1800, the Louisiana Territory was returned to French control. The United States bought the Louisiana Territory from France in 1803.

In 1812, the southern part of the Louisiana Territory was made the state of Louisiana. The northern part, including Arkansas, became the Missouri Territory. In 1817. the U.S. government established Fort Smith to keep peace among Indian tribes in the region. Settlements soon sprang between Arkansas

Post and Fort Smith. In 1819, the government created the Arkansas Territory. It included present-day Arkansas and part of what is now Oklahoma and northeast Texas.

Spotlight: Miller County, Arkansas Territory, A disputed area

Miller County was a county that existed from April 1, 1820 to 1838, first as part of Arkansas Territory and later the State of Arkansas. It included much of what is NOW southeastern Oklahoma and the NOW northeastern counties in Texas (Bowie, Red River, Lamar, Fannin, Cass, Morris, Titus, Franklin, Hopkins, Delta and Hunt). It was named for James Miller, the first governor of the Arkansas Territory. Because early pioneers had already settled and established homes in this area in the 1800's, politicians unknowingly set the peoples and cultures against each other, contributing to conflict and loss of lives between U.S. pioneers and their families, Mexicans, indigenous and displaced Native Americans and fugitives from the law of both countries.

Ancestors, such as the Yates, Folsom and Shelton families, who later married into the Haddock family were already living in and around Miller County in the early 1800's. Although settlers continued to move into the area, the Treaty of Doak's Stand (October 18, 1820) was about to change Miller County.

The Treaty of Doak's Stand, also known as Treaty with the Choctaw, was signed on October 18, 1820 (proclaimed on January 8, 1821) between the United States and the Choctaw Indian tribe. Based on the terms of the accord, the Choctaw agreed to give up approximately one-half of their remaining Choctaw homeland (in Mississippi). In October 1820, Andrew Jackson and Thomas Hinds were sent as commissioners who represented the United States to negotiate a treaty to surrender a portion of Choctaw country in Mississippi. They met with tribal representatives at Doak's Stand on the Natchez Trace, including the chiefs Pushmataha, Mushulatubbee, and Apuckshunubbee, who represented the three major regional divisions of the Choctaw. Chiefs of the towns and other prominent men accompanied them, such as Colonel Silas Dinsmore.

After Doak's Stand, Choctaws had already been moving into the area of Arkansas Territory, but a treaty signed January 20, 1825, ceded the land west of a line "one hundred paces east of Fort Smith, and running thence, due south, to Red river" to them in exchange for their land in the East. The residents of Miller County signed petitions, the territorial government pressured Washington, but all to no avail. Finally, on October 17, 1828, the territorial legislature abolished Miller County NORTH of the Red River and added the remnant of that county east of the new boundary line to Sevier County. The remaining residents burned the courthouse at Miller Court House and all the records.

The commissioners moved the county seat to Jonesborough plantation SOUTH of the Red River (into Texas) on October 23, 1832, and the Miller Court House post office relocated there. However, Miller County south of the Red River was in dispute with the Mexican government. After Texas seceded, they attempted to enforce their claims to the area. In 1838, Texas formed Fannin County, and Washington finally discontinued the Miller Court House post office on December 28, 1838. When Texas joined the Union in 1845 the borders became permanent.

After his proposal to exchange Choctaw land for territory in present-day Arkansas, Pushmataha accused Jackson of deceiving them of the quality of land west of the Mississippi. Pushmataha said, "I know the country well ... The grass is everywhere very short ... There are but few beavers, and the honey and fruit are rare things." Jackson finally resorted to threats to pressure the Choctaw to sign a treaty. He shouted, "Many of your nation are already beyond the Mississippi, and others are every year removing .... If you refuse ... the nation will be destroyed." On October 18, 1820, the chiefs signed the treaty.

The *Treaty of Dancing Rabbit Creek* was a treaty signed on September 27, 1830 (and proclaimed on February 24, 1831) between the Choctaw and the United States Government. This was the first 'removal treaty' carried into effect under the Indian Removal Act. The treaty ceded about 11 million acres of the Choctaw Nation (now Mississippi) in exchange for about 15 million acres in the Indian territory (now the state of Oklahoma). The principal Choctaw negotiators were Chief Greenwood LeFlore, *Musholatubbee*, and *Nittucachee*; the U.S. negotiators were Colonel John Coffee and Secretary of War John Eaton.

The site of the signing of this treaty is in the southwest corner of Noxubee County; the site was known to the Choctaw as Bok Chukfi Ahilha (creek "bok" rabbit "chukfi" place to dance "a+hilha" or Dancing Rabbit Creek). The Treaty of Dancing Rabbit Creek was the last major land cession treaty signed by the Choctaw. With ratification by the U.S. Congress in 1831, the treaty allowed those Choctaw who chose to remain in Mississippi to become the first major non-European ethnic group to gain recognition as U.S. citizens.

Therefore, ancestors who were more adventurous, took risks of life and loss of ownership of land they developed while other ancestors, who followed closely behind established government, could obtain relatively cheap land as the Native Americans were relocated.

A quote from Leven E Moore, summed up the difficulties early settlers had from the disputed territory of Miller County:

> "During a period of 50 years, I have seen many changes….paid taxes to three governments, two states and three counties without changing my place of residence."

> He goes on to say, "When I arrived in Texas in November, 1836, I found living at that time within the present limits of Lamar County about 16 families and 4 or 5 young men without families." (McCuistion)

Arkansas Indians

Indians lived in the Arkansas region for several hundred years before white people arrived. Early white explorers found three principal tribes -- the Caddo, Osage and Quapaw -- in the region. Choctaw, Chickasaw, and Cherokee were later forced to relocate to the Arkansas/Oklahoma area as white settlers took more land in their migration west. During this time and in this place, white people also intermarried with the native Americans. Oral history has it that the Yates family married into the Cherokees and there is some documentation that the Shelton family married native Americans. Apparently, both families, Sheltons and Yates were negatively affected by the treaties as they lost claim to the land they had already settled.

After ceding nearly 11,000,000 acres, the Choctaw emigrated in three stages: the first in the fall of 1831, the second in 1832 and the last in 1833. The Treaty of Dancing Rabbit Creek was ratified by the U.S. Senate on February 25, 1830, and the U.S. President Andrew Jackson was anxious to make it a model of removal.

The Choctaw Trail of Tears was the relocation of the Choctaw Nation from their country referred to now as the Deep South (Alabama, Arkansas, Mississippi, and Louisiana) to lands west of the Mississippi River in Indian Territory in the 1830s. A Choctaw minko (chief) was quoted by the Arkansas Gazette that the removal was a "trail of tears and death." After removal the Choctaws became three distinct groups, the Choctaw Nation of Oklahoma, Jena Band of Choctaw Indians, and the Mississippi Band of Choctaw Indians. (www.wikepedia.org/millercounty, n.d.)

In 1838, Aug, some 12,000 Cherokee Indians in 13 ragtag parties followed the Trail of Tears on a 116-day journey west 800 miles to eastern Oklahoma. Estimates have placed the death toll in camps and in transit as high as 4,000. They followed the trail already set by the Choctaw out of Mississippi, the Creek from Alabama, the Chickasaw from Arkansas and Mississippi, and the Seminole from Florida.

The Muskogee tribe and consequently Cooshattas were a branch of kin to the Choctaws, Chickasaws and Seminoles. The Choctaws were moved principally from Mississippi to the reservation which the government had purchased for them from the Quapaws, in the early 1830's. They were moved up Red river in boats under government contracts, and were landed at or near Fort Towson on the Oklahoma side of the river. In 1836 about five hundred of the Choctaws had some misunderstanding with the national government about their location in the Indian Territory and refused to go there until the adjustment could be made. They landed on the Texas side of the river or crossed over after they had been landed and camped for several months on Bee Bayou just east of Pattonville.

Fort Towson was established in 1824 in response to a need to quell conflicts between lawless elements, American Indian peoples, and settlers claiming the area as part of Arkansas Territory. The fort also served as an outpost on the border between the United States and Texas, which at that time was part of Mexico. Connected to the East by road, Fort Towson served as a gateway for settlers bound for Texas during the 1830s. Those passing through the area included Sam Houston, Davy Crockett, and Stephen F. Austin. When the Choctaw and Chickasaw were displaced from their lands in the southeastern United States, the fort served as a point of dispersal upon their arrival in the west.

Our ancestors were living in this area during this time. Jesse Shelton and William Yates both signed the petition appealing the decision of Washington to trade Miller County land to the Indians. The result of the treaty was to displace both U. S. settlers and the Indians. Miller County residents had to move, and in some cases, were forcibly removed by the military. This contributed to the Yates and Shelton families moving down into Texas. The following article attests to this:

"Jesse Shelton came originally from Kentucky and settled at or near old Ft. Towson when that region was a part of Arkansas. When the government of the United States ceded that section of the Arkansas territory to the Indians all the American settlers who had lodged there were required to move. Mr. Shelton was not long in determining what he would do; he came over to Texas in 1837 and settled down near Roxton having previously built a house which had all of the appurtenances of a fort and for two years kept his family inside that structure. The Indians were giving so much trouble that it was necessary for the few settlers in that locality at that time to work their farms in companies. Some would work and other scout or stand guard.

Shelton's Fort was a refuge to all of his few neighbors for those two troublesome years. After that time the tide of savagery was rolled back further west and it was only now and then that they would escape the vigilance of the Rangers and make a foray into the settlements. The Yates family lived near here and intermarried with the Sheltons.

Captain Shelton was an old Indian fighter and his wife was part Choctaw. He had been living in the Arkansas territory since the very earliest of the 20's and was so familiar with the methods and practices of Indian warfare that he never suffered at their hands. After the county was organized he was for many years connected with courts and congressional commissions and was also a justice of the peace for several years. He died in the year 1854 in his sixty-eighth year. He left a large family all of whom made good citizens. His son, Capt. E. J. Shelton, however, deserves special mention because of both his prominence as a citizen and the conspicuous role he played in the stirring scenes of pioneer days. When he was only 15 years of age he entered the service as a frontier Ranger (early Texas Ranger) and served the Republic of Texas. He was a magnificent horseman, a bold and daring rider, a courageous and fearless Ranger. The settlements were secure only when policed by such heroic bands of men as that to which Eli Shelton belonged. He was married to Miss Martha Ann Elizabeth Yates in 1846, was a farmer by occupation but served his county in the State legislature from 1857, at intervals when not in the war, until 1873.

When the civil war came on he promptly answered his country's call and was in the line of duty in various capacities until the surrender. (1921)

Family legend has it that the Texas Haddocks have Cherokee Indian blood through the Yates family. Cherokee Nation citizenship does not require a specific blood quantum. It does require that you have at least one direct Cherokee ancestor listed on the Dawes Final Rolls, a federal census of those living in the Cherokee Nation that was used to allot Cherokee land to individual citizens in preparation for Oklahoma statehood. However, this has not yet been documented (another good project for the serious researcher).

Detour Spotlight: _Philip Alexander Hattox (Alias, Phil Coe)_

Unknown to many and of special note is an ancestor who came to Texas very early. A son of Moses Hattox (or Haddox) and Admiral Haddock's (b. 1774) grandson, from Georgia was Philip Alexander Hattox. He reportedly killed a man in Georgia and fled to Texas to escape prosecution in 1828-29. He changed his last name from Hattox to Coe, taking on his mother's maiden name. Being a widower at the time, he took his son and 3 daughters with him, stopping briefly in Alabama to visit his uncle (dad's brother) while on his way to Texas. He immediately remarried when in Texas. This makes him the first Haddock that re-located to Texas: Philip Alexander Haddox, alias, Philip Coe.

Philip Hattox was a respected citizen (until the murder) in Upson County, GA in the 1820's. He was married, even though we have no information on his first wife, had a family and was Captain of a Military District and landowner.

Philip Hattox was described to be a man about six feet tall, dark hair, grey eyes and a little bow legged. He could read and write and had a way with words even though he stuttered. He must have had a quick temper which was not always good. To quote Carl Robert Coe, a family researcher, Philip was "a man in every sense of the word…he did not while his time away over the tea table, not as long as the whiskey was within a day's ride…he was a handsome devil and the women liked his style." [Carl Robert Coe "Gone to Texas"]

Once in Texas and living a new life under an alias, Phil Coe apparently lived within the law and became a Texas hero. To add to the intrigue, his neighbor on the adjoining farm in Washington County, Texas was a William R. Pipkin, an ancestor of Elsie Marie Pipkin who married my dad, **William Marvin Haddock** Therefore, we had a Haddock (Haddox) and a Pipkin living in Texas before the territory became a state and they played a major part in making Texas history. Lastly, William R Pipkin's son married one of Phil Coe's daughters! So my mother and dad were not the first Haddock/Pipkin union. Both Haddock and Pipkin received land from the Republic of Texas for migrating early and are included in Austin's 300, members of the original settlers founded by Moses Austin and his son, Stephen F. Austin.

The best reason I can find that William R Pipkin came to Texas from Tennessee is that he may have known Thomas Jones Hardeman, whom founded what became know as Hardeman County, Tennessee, fought in the War of 1812, and moved to Texas to help in the war of independence. It was reported he and his brothers Thomas Jones and Blackstone Hardeman and his sister Julia Ann Bacon, together with their families (all related), numbering about twenty-five people in all, moved to Texas in the fall of 1835. (Frances W Wilson, March, 1986). Reportedly, he also helped name the Capitol of Texas as 'Austin.'

The second best reason for William R Pipkin coming to Texas was that he was part of the Cherokee Indian Wars, involving the Indian Removal Act and forced removal of Cherokee people from their native lands to Indian Territory in what is now, Oklahoma. He may have heard the stories of the conflict in Texas and free or cheap land to be obtained.

These stories are very interesting and worth the effort to research further for a serious student of family history. Other Haddox and Pipkin ancestors also migrated to Texas probably due to the reports of cheap land and opportunity in Texas. The state operated under the Headright system offering a 'league (over 4,000 acres) and a labor (over 177 acres)' of land to every married man who brought cattle to Texas. Evidence of this can be found in the Mt. Zion Cemetery, Hopkins County, Texas where many ancestors are buried. Two people with Haddox as the last name are buried there also.

More Family History

Meanwhile, the area around Batesville, Arkansas was settled by several Haddock family members, which is evidenced by gravesites in several cemeteries. A family cemetery, designated as "Haddock Cemetery" by the local genealogical society, has several gravesites identified and many others are unmarked. The old unfenced cemetery is located near Batesville in an open pasture and is protected by a large grove of trees.

It is here in the Batesville area that we find **Jordan Haddock** and his family from whom this line of Haddocks descended.

Focus: Jordan David Haddock (1805-1861)

When Jordan David Haddock was born in 1805 in Chicod, North Carolina, his father, Nasby 'Hall', was 19 and his mother, Sarah, was 17.

Occupation

1850 Census reports farmer, but no land value listed, which probably meant he was a sharecropper farmer.[3] First time this shows up.

He married Sarah Clementine 'Clemmie' BUCK in 1829 in Pitt County, North Carolina. They had 13 children in 21 years. Their first 10 children were born in North Carolina, while the last 3 children were born in Arkansas. He died on March 18, 1861, in Batesville, Arkansas, at the age of 56, and was buried in Sulphur Rock, Arkansas.

----

[3] A sharecropper is a tenant farmer, someone who works land that's rented from its owner.

As stated, they lived around the Buck family & there were at least two generations of Bucks who married Haddocks and made the trip all the way to Texas, eventually.

Residence

Jordan David Haddock lived in Pitt County, North Carolina, in 1830, 1840, and by the 1850 Census (in his mid-40's), he had moved to St Francis, Arkansas (probably moved in 1849). By 1860, Jordan David Haddock lived in the Gainsburro Township, Independence County, Arkansas.

The Night the Stars Fell

So, in 1833 Jordan David Haddock was still living in North Carolina where they may have witnessed one of the most spectacular meteor showers in history on "the night the stars fell." "A tempest of falling stars broke over the Earth. The sky was scored in every direction with shining tracks and illuminated with majestic fireballs. At Boston, the frequency of meteors was estimated to be about half that of flakes of snow in an average snowstorm. Their numbers... were quite beyond counting; but as it waned, a reckoning was attempted, from which it was computed, on the basis of that much-diminished rate, that 240,000 must have been visible during the nine hours they continued to fall." – (Agnes Clerke's, Victorian Astronomy Writer)

Birth of Children

His daughter Harriet Ann was born on March 16, 1832, in Pitt County, North Carolina. Harriet Ann Haddock -1832–1865

His daughter Elizabeth Clementine "Clemmy" was born on April 13, 1833, in Pitt County, North Carolina. Elizabeth Clementine "Clemmy" Haddock - 1833–1917

His daughter Louisa Elizabeth was born in April 1833 in Pitt County, North Carolina. Louisa Elizabeth Haddock Buck - 1833–1910

His son Ransom "Ranse" was born in 1834 in Pitt County, North Carolina. Ransom "Ranse" Haddock - 1834–1863

His son Lanier Lorenzo "Lonzo" was born in 1839 in Pitt County, North Carolina. Lanier Lorenzo "Lonzo" Haddock - 1839–1938 Other Haddocks went by the name, Lonzo or Alonzo, with several showing up in Haddock, Georgia, these being descendants of Admiral (b. 1753).

His son Jordan David was born on October 22, 1840, in Pitt County, North Carolina. Jordan David Haddock - 1840–1880

His son Noah Uriah was born in 1843 in Pitt County, North Carolina. Noah Uriah Haddock - 1843–1900

His son **Calvin Cash** was born on December 7, 1845, in Chicod, North Carolina. Calvin Cash Haddock - 1845–1927

His daughter Clessonie was born in 1848 in Pitt County, North Carolina. Clessonie Haddock - 1848–1924

His daughter Clenny (Clemmy) was born in 1848 in Pitt County, North Carolina. Clenny (Clemmy) Haddock - 1848–1907

His son William Pleas was born on April 17, 1851. William Pleas Haddock - 1851–1930

His daughter Lucinda "Lou" was born in 1852. Lucinda "Lou" Haddock - 1852–1894

His son Hiram was born in 1853. Hiram Haddock - 1853–1860

Death

Jordan David Haddock died on March 18, 1861, in Batesville, Arkansas, when he was 56 years old and was buried at Liberty Cemetery. (See Appendix VII)

Son, **Calvin Cash Haddock** was born December 7, 1845 in North Carolina. Around 1849, Calvin moved with his parents in a two-wheeled ox cart to St. Francis County, Arkansas, where his mother is said to have died. After three or four years there, it is believed they moved to the Batesville, Arkansas area in Independence County. Jordan reportedly deeded the land to the Liberty Church and cemetery in the area around 1854, which suggests he owned land there. This is the area where Calvin resided until 1900, when he moved his own family to Texas.

Spotlight: The American Civil War

At age 19, Calvin, enlisted in Company E of the 45th Arkansas Calvary, Confederate States of America in Independence County. It was during the Spring of 1864, three years after his dad's death. Calvin was in active duty 14 months under the command of Colonel Baker and Captain Jim Fetzer. Later, he was transferred to Colonel McRea's Brigade, Fagan's Division.

In 1864, General Sterling Price tried to recapture Missouri for the South in a daring raid. Calvin Haddock, a private in the Calvary saw action in this raid and was wounded in the leg. General Price's forces were defeated at Westport, which is part of present-day Kansas City. Price's defeat marked the end of full scale fighting in the state (The World Book Encyclopedia, 1979a). Private Haddock surrendered to the Northern forces on May 11, 1865, and was paroled on June 5, 1865 at Jacksonport, Arkansas.

Private Haddock must have been well-liked by his friends. For example, in an affidavit on the application for his soldier's pension, one of Calvin's friends who served with him wrote: "we rode together, ate together (when we had anything to eat), we fought together, bled together, and would have died together...." (See documents in Appendix ------- for supporting evidence).

The Civil War split families apart and positioned relatives fighting on opposite sides. The Haddock family was not exempt from this situation because Greenberry Haddock, son of Zachariah, was a Union soldier.

It is reported that a group of Federal troops, mostly from the First Arkansas Cavalry, ranged over Barry County hunting down and killing men they believed to have been Confederate sympathizers. John Ireland, son-in-law of Zachariah Haddock, was killed in his own home near Cassville by these Federals, leaving Mary, his widow, to rear her small children alone.

This destruction, added to that of the Bushwhackers, left most of the Missouri and Arkansas settlers destitute. With their homes and livestock destroyed and land grown up in weeds, rebuilding was a monumental task. Anyone showing sudden affluence was suspected of having been a bushwhacker and ill feelings grew up between families, friends, and neighbors. A number of Haddocks left the Arkansas-Missouri area shortly after the Civil War, going mostly to Kansas, Oklahoma and Texas. Others remained and rebuilt in their old locations.

Medicine during the American Civil War

During the American Civil War, Calvin Cash Haddock was a soldier who likely required medical treatment.

Some ancestors, who were already in Texas at the time of the Civil War, served on the side of the Confederacy. For example, the Shelton family were early pioneers who provided men who served. The one who held the most rank was William Harvey Shelton, who was appointed brigadier general of the Lamar County area (9th Militia Brigade) by Governor Clark on June 17, 1861. Because of poor communications, there was some dispute over who was actively holding that position, so he only served briefly before politics won out and another person was appointed to the same position. Military correspondence in the state archives are available to document these events. He died of ill health before the war was over and is buried near Honey Grove. Eli Jennings (or Jenway) Shelton also served in the Confederacy, holding the rank of Captain in the 9th Texas Infantry. He fought in Corinth, Mississippi and Fredericksburg, Virginia and lived through it. A brother, Ervin Shelton, was a private in the 9th Brigade was killed in the battle of Vicksburg.

The Yates family, who intermarried with the Sheltons and were in Texas early, also had ancestors who fought and died. Albert G. Yates was in Company G of the 9th Regiment, Texas Calvary and was killed in the battle of Elkhorn Tavern at Pea Ridge, Arkansas. After his death, his brother, Thomas Keelan (Keeling) Yates, a direct maternal ancestor, joined at the age of 32 and left behind his wife and several children. He served in the 19th Regiment, Texas Calvary was killed probably somewhere near Nashville Tennessee. His wife died soon thereafter and their children were raised by the Eli Shelton family (who had married one of the Yates women). The search continues for details of Thomas K. Yates and his wife's death.

Religion and Rituals

While English immigrants may have been Catholic, most of the American Haddocks were of the Protestant faith and the greater percent of them were Baptist, until they showed up in Texas, where the Methodists were active evangelists. John Wesley, himself, came to the South and evangelized, spreading the Methodist denomination in America. Beginning with the Haddock brothers who reportedly landed in Maine, they were described as devout Protestants who took their religion seriously, even though many of the early explorers to America were more adventurous and less religious.

Arkansas during the Reconstruction Era

Following the American Civil War, Calvin Cash Haddock lived in Arkansas, when life during the Reconstruction Era was full of uncertainty.

Calvin reportedly professed faith in the Son of God at the age of 21 and united with the Presbyterian church, but later in life united with the Methodist church and from the day of his conversion remained faithful to the Christian faith.

Besides his Civil War service, we can look at his obituary and other available records to learn how Calvin Haddock lived his life. Calvin married Miss Virginia Elizabeth NESBIT in Independence County, Arkansas on December 30, 1866. Mrs. Haddock was born on April 1, 1849, a native of Tennessee, but reportedly moved to Arkansas with her parents prior to 1850. They lived on adjoining farms to the Haddock household and it was there the romance, which culminated in marriage, started between this couple. It seems this was common in those days. They had eleven children: four died as infants and two married daughters died, with all being buried at Bethel near Batesville (see Appendix VII). Death of infants and/or their mothers was very common in those days and the Haddocks were not immune from it. Apparently, Virginia's dad died while she was young because he is not listed on the 1850 Census (see appendices at end for more on the Nesbits). As mentioned, Calvin's parents also died while he was young.

Focus: Calvin Cash Haddock (1845-1927)

When Calvin Cash Haddock was born on December 7, 1845, in Chicod, North Carolina, his father, Jordan, was 40 and his mother, Sarah, was 33.

He married Virginia Elizabeth NESBITT on December 30, 1866. This would have been after his Civil War service. They had 12 children in 26 years. All of their children were born in Arkansas, even though they eventually moved to Texas. He died on February 28, 1927, in Commerce, Texas, at the age of 81, and was buried there.

Residences

1850 Cache, St Francis, Arkansas

Calvin Cash Haddock lived in Gainsboro, Arkansas, in 1860 at age 16.

Calvin Cash Haddock lived in Gainsboro, Arkansas, in 1870 at age 24 and stayed there raising a family all the way through the 1900 Census. By 1910, he lived in Justice Precinct 4, Hopkins, Texas and by 1920 he lived in Commerce, Texas.

Occupation

At 35, listed his occupation as farmer, then at 55, farmer and still owed a mortgage, at 65, farmer and owned his land free & clear, at 75, public school janitor and worked there until his death.

Marriage

As stated, Calvin Cash Haddock married Virginia Elizabeth Nesbitt on December 30, 1866, when he was 21 years old. Virginia Elizabeth Nesbitt lived to be about 88. (1849–1937)

Children

His daughter Margaret A. V. was born on January 10, 1868. She passed away on January 15, 1868, in Batesville, Arkansas, at less than a year old.

His daughter Cordelia Carolina was born on April 25, 1869, in Batesville, Arkansas. She passed away on October 25, 1872, in Batesville, Arkansas, at the age of 3.

His daughter Lilly M. was born in 1870. She passed away in 1880 in Batesville, Arkansas, at the age of 10.

His daughter Virginia Elizabeth "Jennie" was born in 1871 in Batesville, Arkansas and died about age 27 in 1898. (1871–1898)

His daughter Louisa Lizziebeth Elizabeth was born on November 11, 1875, in Batesville, Arkansas and died at about age 98. (1875–1973)

His daughter Virginia E. was born in 1876 in Arkansas and died age 99.(1876–1975)

His son Nesbitt was born in December 1881. Nesbitt passed away on August 25, 1884, in Batesville, Arkansas, at the age of 2. -Nesbitt Haddock (1881–1884)

His daughter Tommie Ann was born on December 12, 1882, in Batesville, Arkansas. Tommie Ann Haddock had the greatest longevity dying at age **103**. (1882–1986)

His daughter Ruthy L was born on June 20, 1884. Ruthy L Haddock lived to be about 83. (1884–1967)

His son **William David** (Dave) was born on November 22, 1887, in Batesville, Arkansas, the next direct descendant. William David (Dave) Haddock - 1887–1948

His daughter Kathryn Kate was born on September 2, 1894, in Batesville, Arkansas. Kathryn Kate Haddock lived to be about 95. (1894–1989)

His daughter Virginia Elizabeth "Jennie" passed away in June 1898 in Batesville, Arkansas, at the age of 27. Virginia Elizabeth "Jennie" Haddock - 1871–1898

Death

Calvin Cash Haddock died on February 28, 1927, in Commerce, Texas, when he was 81 years old. He is buried in Rosemond Cemetery there. (See Appendix VIII)

Rosemond Cemetery is a city or government-operated cemetery. In Great Britain, many Haddocks were buried in the churchyard in Essex, or other locales, and our ancestors had to have financial means to have graves marked. As people migrated and settled in the frontier areas of colonial American times, small family plots containing immediate and extended family members were common. You may have noticed the Haddock cemetery in Pitt County, North Carolina, the Liberty Cemetery near Batesville, Arkansas or even the Mt. Zion Cemetery in Hopkins County, Texas. Here people donated land for churches and cemeteries, which assured the continued maintenance of the plots.

The key practice was to have the Church or relatives or a cemetery association maintain the gravesites, not the government. Small cemeteries were located in the corners of private farmland, along wooded areas, or frequently on hilltops overlooking a stream. Land for larger cemeteries were donated to churches and was common until the early 1900's. As the number of small, rural farms declined and land ownership changed through the decades, the locations of small family plots were lost and ultimately forgotten.

During these times, it was customary for neighbors to gather when there was a death in the family. They brought food, helped dig the grave and laid out the corpse in its best clothes. In lieu of embalming, soda was patted onto the faces of the dead to preserve the features until burying time. It was sometimes said of a man that he only wore a necktie twice in his life, once for his wedding and again for his funeral. Friends sat up with the deceased at night before the funeral. At the grave site, lines were taken from the harness and used to gently lower the casket into the grave. Caskets were often made ahead of time and kept in the home until time for use, black walnut being the favorite wood. Frequently, the casket served as a storage place for bedding and clothing. Haddocks, being deft with their hands, nearly always had their caskets ready. They were also in demand to build caskets for others. It seems odd that the Haddock family has been exposed to death a lot, but seems to have learned little about grieving. As a family, we are noted for building things well with our hands, but being rather limited in expressing feelings from the heart, including sorrow.

PART V

The Texas Migration

From the by-laws of the Lamar County Historical Society, I have borrowed a classification system which declared all those who came to the old Red River District (in Texas) before the close of the year 1830 would be classed as **Pathfinders**, while those who came between that date and the close of the year 1850 would be classed as **Pioneers**. Those coming after the close of the year 1870, would be regarded as **old settlers**. (Ed H. McCuistion, October, 1995) Instead of restricting this system to the Red River District, I am applying the classification system to ancestors in general who came to the territory that became Texas. In addition, anyone who came after the close of 1870, I am simply calling, '**Settlers**.'

Using this system, we find **Pathfinders**, such as:

Class of 1817-1818: William Ragsdale & his son, Thomas (who married into the Yates family).

Class of 1820: William Rabb, settled originally near Jonesborough, then moved to Austin's Colony in 1826. His son married into the Ragsdale family.

Class of 1829: Phillip Alexander Hattox, alias Phil Coe, who was a part of Austin's Colony, as was William R Pipkin, both of whom settled in Washington County and are listed as among Austin's Colony (Austin's 300) and their descendents

In Native American spirituality, the wolf is symbolic of pathfinder and teacher. It has to do with having a strategy in hunting it's prey and a fierce approach life that is tendered by a family-centered approach. Children of pathfinders in each migration often grew up without the advantages of school and a fair degree of social life. It has been said that the two highest held values of the Pathfinders were their land and their wives.(McCuistion)

Ancestors among the **Pioneers**, include the:

Class of 1834: Thomas Avis Yates and William Yates, who settled in the south part of Lamar County, near Ft. Shelton and their descendents.

Class of 1837: George Washington Helm, Sr. & Ruth Mayo Burnett, whose son, John Jackson was born in Charleston, Delta County during that year and their descendents. Also, married into the Yates family.

Class of 1841: Shadrack W Pipkin and Steward Pipkin and their descendents. Both received Unconditional Certificates for 320 each in Washington County on 13 June, 1844 (had to reside in Texas 3 years to qualify) There are several other Pipkins scattered throughout the land records of that time, which makes another research project for an inspiring family history researcher.

During this time, people went to work establishing educational institutions and, by 1860, several educational schools were advertised in the Paris news. Along these lines, Mayo College was established originally in Cooper, Delta County and moved to Commerce after a fire in 1894.

Many of our ancestors, especially on my mother's side, the Pipkin family, came from Tennessee. In 1860, Texas had received the 3rd most migrants from the state of Tennessee following Arkansas and Missour

Qualifying as an **Old Settler** would be:

Class of 1867, John Burnett Raines, who married into the Yates family and lived in the Branom Community, Hopkins County, Texas where he donated a parcel of land for the Mt. Zion Cemetery.

By the time Calvin Haddock moved to Texas, along with his son, **William David**, problems with the Indians, Mexicans, slaves, lawless, and land disputes had been minimized. With the incorporation of Texas into the Union in 1845 and the support of the United States military, law and order had been brought to Texas. Consequently, the population grew. For example, the 1850 Census estimated Texas population at over 200,000 with growth slowing during the Civil War and over 3 million residents by 1900.

Settler, Class of 1900, Calvin Haddock, moved to Texas in 1900 in two covered wagons with five other families. The trip reportedly took 18 days and they had a lot of fun (written communication with Lizzie Haddock Wells). In reviewing the records, it appears that Calvin's sister, Louisa, and her sister-in-law, Mary, with their respective families all settled in the Cooper area. Mary A. Harrington Johnson, widow of Noah Haddock, her children's families, George Washington Haddock and Emma Griffin, and Ella Elizabeth Haddock Davidson and family also accompanied them (Paris newspaper 11/2/1978). Noah died in Batesville, in March, shortly before the group left for Texas. His widow, Mary, who later remarried, a man named George W Johnson moved her family along with Calvin's family and Calvin's sister, Louisa and her husband, William A. Buck. It was reported by Tommie Haddock Moore that Louisa's husband and four children died and were buried in the Charleston cemetery near Cooper.

These names and dates all have been checked, except the Bucks who were buried in the Charleston Cemetery. Reminder, while Louisa married a Buck, her mother also was from the Buck family.

How they got there

Many of the Pathfinders, earliest settlers, flat-boated by river to Texas. These boats were called 'keelboats.' It's possible some continued to Texas by horseback and/or wagons following the Southwest Trail, as previously mentioned. Alternatively, they could have followed the Cherokee Trace which was well-worn and became a historic trail that traversed East and Northeast Texas. The Cherokee Indians are credited with blazing this route about 1821. It is also possible that the trace may have evolved from one marked by other Native American groups or French traders a century earlier and that the Cherokees further defined and smoothed out this course. According to folklore, the Indians dragged buffalo skins behind their horses to flatten the tall grass and then cleared the path of brush and logs. They charted a road that encountered the best camping places, river fords, and springs. They also planted honeysuckle and rose bushes along the route. The white blooming hedgerows functioned as bright and effective indicators of the trace, and the stiff branches and briars of the Cherokee rose later became noted by settlers as a dependable shrub for fencing.

The trail ran from the vicinity of Nacogdoches north through Northeast Texas including present-day Gregg, Upshur, and Camp counties. The road then crossed Big Cypress Creek into Titus County near the historic location of Fort Sherman and continued north to Indian settlements in Oklahoma and Arkansas. Serving as a travel and trading route for East Texas Indians, the trail also enabled the migration of many settlers into Texas. Popular tradition holds that Sam Houston, David Crockett, and other participants in the Texas Revolution first crossed the Red River into Texas on the Cherokee Trace. There was a ferry operating at Jonesborough, near the Kiamichi River before 1820. Early land grant surveys of the 1830s and 1840s mention the trail as a landmark and also reference roads that subsequently evolved from this route such as the Fort Towson Road and Clarksville-Nacogdoches Road. In 1839, after their defeat at the battle of the Neches, many Cherokees fled Texas on this trail. Remnants of the old Cherokee Trace along with hedgerows of roses can still be found in Northeast Texas today.

Indians in Texas

There were many Indians living in Texas during the time of Texas independence. Most significant were the Comanches. However it wasn't until 1836 that settlers began to realize how big a problem they really were.

It started with the Parker massacre in May 1836 when the Comanches attacked the Parker family at Fort Parker near present day Mexia, without any warning and killed and kidnapped several members of the family. The, now famous, Cynthia Ann Parker was the most known. Rachel Parker Palmer, who was also taken captive, journaled her experiences in detail, giving the rest of the pioneers a glimpse into the barbaric practices of this tribe.

The Mexican government, and before them, the Spanish, knew. However, they weren't sharing information with the Texas settlers. From G.C. Gwynne 's book, Empire of the Summer Moon, we learned they may have been using Texas pioneers to create a buffer between them and the Comanches.

The Spanish knew that the Comanches had developed from a dull, primitive tribe to a strong, vengeful, clever people from 1625 to the mid-1750's, through adapting and using the horse, brought over from Spain. Without the mustang, a desert horse, they probably would have remained Stone Age hunters. By the early 1600's, wild mustangs had spread all the way up to what is now, New Mexico.

Apaches were raiding in New Mexico by the mid-1650's and all Indians in Texas had horses by 1700. Horses were the new technology of that time. However, the Comanches were the only tribe to learn to fight from horseback. And they became experts at it.

Because of their expertise, they developed a striking range for raids up to 400 miles. They were difficult to catch when they would raid, kill, rape, mutilate, and run away with captives by riding all night and keeping so much distance between their camp and their victims. They were also good traders, selling buffalo hides, stolen horses, and captives and buying guns, ammunition, and food.

The Comanches stalled migration of Texas settlers for several years after it became a republic. The border was, essentially where the wooded land ended and the Texas prairies began. This would be around Ft. Worth, south to Waco, then westward toward San Antonio.

Consequently, some people settled in East Texas and didn't move west until later, if at all. People who did were like the PARKER family: Calvinistic, righteous, hard-nosed, and audacious. Some said they were God-fearing people and had little fear left over for the Indians. Taken as a child, Cynthia Ann became integrated into the Comanche band and married, having at least two children. When first found living among the Comanches and given a chance to leave, she declined.

While many ancestors stopped in Delta County, near Charleston, Calvin moved his own family to Hopkins county. From Hopkins County, Calvin and family then moved to Commerce. They lived for one year in this residence, which formerly stood where the old post office building that was converted to a public library now stands. From that location, they then moved to a house on Main street, where he lived until he died. A granddaughter remembered that he would ride a train from Commerce on Saturday afternoon to visit them. He would walk from the train to their house north, of the Mt. Zion cemetery in the Branom Community, carrying an umbrella. He would raise the umbrella up as a signal and the grandchildren would run up to him and hug him. He would bring them candy and chewing gum from town. Virginia, his wife, seldom came to visit. She was reported to be the one in the family with a negative attitude and an angry disposition. One relative said it this way, "she was real mean and he was a real good man and did whatever she wanted."

Calvin, on the other hand, was recognized as one of the community's best citizens, a worthy confederate veteran, a faithful member of the Masonic fraternity, a consistent Christian, a good husband and a kind and exemplary father. He was apparently well-known by many adults and children, who had learned to love him during his sixteen years of faithful service as janitor at the local school building.

Upon his death, the funeral service was conducted by Rev. George C. French of Greenville, former pastor and assisted by Rev. C.A. Long, pastor of the local Methodist church. Professor A.L. Day, school superintendent, also made a very appropriate talk. "He dignified labor," Professor Day said. "He loved his work. He was one of the most cheerful workers I have ever known. Considerate and kind to the children; I always knew they were well cared for and protected when Mr. Haddock was around," the superintendent said. "He was not a man to complain and find fault, but was ever helpful to his associates and always had an encouraging word for all. Although 82 years of age when he answered the summons of death, he retained the cheerful optimistic spirit of his youth and radiated good cheer, helping wherever he came in contact with others."

One of the surviving children was quoted as saying, "I never knew my father to strike one of the children in anger. He was always gentle, kind, cheerful and happy," in talking about the life of her father.

The details of his last hours of life were recorded in the obituary. He was apparently at work at the school when suffering a stroke or heart attack. Professor Day reported that he called out to Calvin as he was about to leave the building, "I'm going home now, Mr. Haddock." Instead of the familiar "Alright, professor," from Mr. Haddock in answer to this daily good-bye, Mr. Day heard a groan. Consequently, he immediately made an investigation, having to inspect three rooms before he found Mr. Haddock, where he had fallen to the floor shortly before closing time. In about ten minutes, his day's work would have been finished. Professor Day had him carried home and he never rallied from the stroke.

The report continued by saying that on Saturday he appeared better and asked for food. He recognized his relatives and talked with them. On Saturday afternoon, his condition grew worse, and watchers at the bedside came to know that he was nearing the valley of the shadow of death. The end came at 12:05 Monday.

When Calvin died, he left behind a widow and several grown children, including a daughter, Tommie Haddock Moore and a son, **William David Haddock**, the next direct descendent in our family line (His wife's mother was a Yates). It was Dave's sister, Tommie, who surfaces as having the most longevity in the family, living to be **103** years old. Born in Independence County, Arkansas in 1882, Tommie Haddock came to Texas, when she was 18 or 19 years old, via a covered wagon. She said that she remembers her own mother, Virginia Nesbit Haddock, raised her to work and to be nice to people. She was quoted in a Paris, Texas newspaper article, written when she was 101 years old, as saying, "I was raised that way and I haven't departed from it."

Other newspaper quotes: "When you get old, you like the children. The little children (great-grand kids) come here so pretty and nice and I just want to nurse them you know. With my own children, I never had time to do that because I worked all the time to keep everything in its place." Advice for mothers, "Stay at home with your children and keep house."

Quotes taken by Maredia Haddock Cunningham at a visit before her death, given as sayings from her mother (Virginia Nesbit Haddock):

"Some women can throw more out the window with a spoon than a man can bring in the door with a shovel."

"Always tell it like it is no matter who it hurts."

"If you have a pain, forget it, get busy, lock it out of your mind, and don't lay down and nurse it and it will go away."

She lived at Cherry Street Manor (nursing home) in Paris, Texas the last years of her life and died at 103 years old in May, 1986. I visited her in March, 1986 shortly before her death. At that time, she was still very sharp in her thinking and showed a distinct sparkle in her eyes. She lived in Hopkins County, near Cumby, most of her life in Texas. She is buried in Rosemound Cemetery, Commerce, Texas.

Her brother, William David, is our direct ancestor in this Texas line of Haddocks.

Focus: William David Haddock (1887-1948)

When William David (Dave) Haddock was born on November 22, 1887, in Batesville, Arkansas, his father, Calvin, was 41 and his mother, Virginia, was 38.

He married Flora Gertrude "Trudy" RAINES and they had six children together, 5 survived to adulthood. All their children were born in Texas, although different counties. Trudy's mother, Martha "Mattie" YATES was a member of the Yates family, whose ancestors moved into Lamar County, Texas while it was still a territory of Mexico. Her ancestors survived the hostilities of Native Americans, both indigenous and displaced, as well as the lawlessness that prevails in a region yet undefined by governmental forces, and made a life for themselves. Mattie Yates lost her father in the Civil War and her mother shortly after that, leaving her and siblings to be raised by her aunt and uncle, the Eli J Shelton family.

Residence

William David (Dave) Haddock lived in Gainsboro, Arkansas, in 1900 before making the move to Texas with his dad, Calvin.

In 1910, they lived in Justice Precinct 4, Hopkins, Texas

The 1920 Census finds him married, head of house, living in Justice Precinct 4, Hopkins, Texas

In 1930, they lived in Precinct 1, Hunt County, Texas

William David (Dave) Haddock lived with his family in rural Hopkins County, Texas, in 1935.

William David (Dave) Haddock lived in Delta County, Texas, on April 1, 1940 and lived in Klondike, Texas, in 1942.

Occupation

At 23, listed farmer, but rented. At 33, and at 42, farmed, but rented land.

Education: Claimed completed 2nd year of college.

1st Marriage

William David (Dave) Haddock married Flora Gertrude "Trudy" RAINES on November 22, 1908, in Hopkins County, Texas, when he was 21 years old.

Flora Gertrude "Trudy" Raines - 1891–1921. She was born in Hopkins County, Texas, the daughter of John Allen Raines of Kentucky and Martha Elizabeth "Mattie" Yates of Lamar County, Texas. They lived in the Branom Community, near the west side of Hopkins County. As stated, Mattie Yates' family dates to early settlers of Texas through William Yates, one of the original landowners in Lamar County, Texas, and Thomas Avis Yates, who fought in the volunteer Texas army in the campaign of Bexar, 1835, and his son, Thomas Keelin Yates, her father, who died in the Civil War.

Birth of Children

Dave's daughter Zoia Avaline was born on August 1, 1909, in Hopkins County, Texas. Zoia Avaline Haddock was about 99. (1909–2008)

His son **William Marvin** was born on August 28, 1910, in Hopkins County, Texas. **William Marvin Haddock** was 55. Cause of death: cancer. (1910–1965)

His daughter Juanita Alberta was born on August 21, 1911, in Hopkins County, Texas. Juanita Alberta Haddock was about 99. (1911–2010)

His daughter Mattie Virginia was born on May 9, 1918, in Hopkins County, Texas. Mattie Virginia Haddock was about 95. (1918–2013)

His daughter Minnie Elizabeth was born on February 13, 1919, in Hopkins County, Texas. Minnie Elizabeth Haddock was about 89 when she died. (1919–2008)

His daughter Mamie Ruth was born on May 8, 1920, in Hopkins County, Texas. She passed away on May 29, 1920, in Hopkins County, Texas, at less than a year old, reportedly as the result of an illness from the flu. Mamie Ruth Haddock (1920–1920)

Death of Wife

His wife Flora Gertrude "Trudy" passed away on November 18, 1921, in Hopkins County, Texas, at the age of 30, reportedly as the result of the flu. They had been married 12 years. She is buried along with Mamie Ruth at the Mt. Zion Cemetery in Branom community, Hopkins County, TX.

Registering for the Draft in World War I & II

After the Selective Service Act was signed in May 1917, William David (Dave). Haddock registered for the draft on 09 May 1918, showing his residence as the Branom Community, Hopkins County, TX, USA

Because he was a farmer with a family, he was not called to active duty service.

William David (Dave). Haddock registered for the U.S. military draft in 1942 during World War II. He was never called to active duty service in this conflict either.

2nd Marriage

William David (Dave) Haddock married again. This time to Nunie Mae McMANUS on June 18, 1923, in Commerce, Texas, when he was 35 years old and they had 11 children together. The McManus family were acquainted with the Haddock and Raines family and at least one other ancestor married into their family. Dave died on December 10, 1948, in Commerce, Texas, at the age of 61, and was buried there.

Nunie Mae McManus outlived him and died about age 62. (1905–1967)

Birth of Children

His daughter Margaret Beatrice was born on August 1, 1925. Margaret Beatrice Haddock was about 90 when she died. (1925–2015)

His daughter Helen Louise was born on August 15, 1929, in Texas. Helen Louise Haddock was about 65 when she died. (1929–1994)

His daughter Nelda Myril was born on August 24, 1929, in Hunt County, Texas. Nelda Myril Haddock is still living. (1929- now)

His son W D was born in 1932 in Texas and is still living.

His daughter Zoie Oleta was born on December 17, 1934, in Hopkins County, Texas and recently died at about 82. (1934-2016)

His daughter Mary Oretha was born about 1938, in Texas. Mary Oretha Haddock (1938–living)

His daughter Shirley Jo was born on February 16, 1940, in Hopkins County, Texas. Shirley Jo Haddock was about 50 when she died in a shooting incident. (1940–1990)

His daughter Patricia Mae was born on October 16, 1944, in Petty, Texas. –This was near the Lamar/Fannin County border where the Yates families had land. Patricia Mae Haddock was about 65 when she died. (1944–2009)

Death

William David (Dave) Haddock died on December 10, 1948, in Commerce, Texas, when he was 61 years old and was buried in Rosemound Cemetery. (See Appendix IX)

More on William David Haddock

Very little records have been kept about William David Haddock, so several of his children living at the time of this writing were surveyed to gather information about his personality, appearance and background. He was known to have been favored by his mother, Virginia, and his personality reflected some of her disposition.

William David Haddock had two wives during his life. He reportedly met the first woman he would marry, Flora Gertrude Raines, while attending East Texas Normal College in Commerce, Texas.

A check with the college library reveals that there were no transcripts until 1917 and no yearbook until 1920. Also, there were fires in 1894 when the college was still in Cooper and more after moving to Commerce. If available, they would only be a listing of those who graduated, probably no record of attendance. (for more on the Raines family, who were early Texas settlers, see Appendix ? ----------).

They married when she was about 17 and the first child, Aveline, was born the next year. Apparently, neither one finished college. All together, they had five living children, four girls and one boy (see Appendix). This man was apparently prone to spend several days at a time away from home. It was reported that Dave had a habit of making trips to the Cooper, Texas area. On at least one occasion while he was away, Gertrude left home and took the kids with her to Commerce to be with her parents. She apparently was tired of his spending so much time away from home. He came to

Commerce in the buggy and talked to her into coming back home with the kids. When they got back, she wrote to her mother, "our fine horse was dead."

Apparently, the horse had died due to neglect since he was away and left the care of animals with her not expecting that she would go home to her parents. Gertrude died in 1921, reportedly with blood poisoning following a miscarriage. He reportedly continued his trips to Cooper after her death, leaving the children at home alone. Perhaps this behavior reflects an element of being "stubborn" that is associated with the name of William.

Dave Haddock married Nunie McManus in 1924 and had eight additional children (see Appendix IX). Several of the children from both families were contacted to provide input regarding their father. There was considerable consistency in their reports, although he seemed to mellow somewhat with the second group of children.

The features that stood out in their minds were listed below:

"Good looking, hardworking, neat - always clean, looked nice in all his dressing (up or down), tall & proud, great with outside family - but not that way with the children, I call it two faced."

"His favorite color was blue. He was known to be dressed for the occasion, 'nice & snappy,' usually dressed in a shirt, tie and suit."

Regarding his habits and personality, he was not known to travel much. Perhaps because he never had the money, but his travel was mostly restricted to visiting with relatives in their homes. He seemed to visit friends more while his first wife was living, perhaps because she was closer to his own age and his second wife was much younger.

He had some family pets as well as hogs, milk cows, horses and mules, as was the case of many people those days.

His nickname was "Colonel" when he was younger, "Dave" when he was older, "daddy" to his children and "papaw" to his grandchildren. He was known to laugh and play practical jokes, but mostly away from home. He was known to have an occasional beer with friends, but didn't drink excessively, perhaps, again, because of limited finances.

He was known to have common sense "at times" and he called it "horse sense." He was quoted as saying that "without common sense, book sense was no good." This seems to still hold true today.

He was "definitely" seen as a perfectionist and everyone around him had to be "or else." But this part of him was viewed as a virtue by at least one daughter and she said she strongly practiced it herself. He was also seen as being very bossy.

Regarding his ability to manage the family finances, there were mixed views ranging from "yes" to " no" to "not bad." Other comments included the following: "he could stretch a dollar and he could always find good bargains and get more with his money than most people I know." "He had good taste, and loved nice things in the home or to wear."

A daughter quoted his father-in-law, Grandpa Raines, as saying, "He would buy a steamboat 1000 miles from water if he could get it on credit." Another daughter stated he was too free with his money. But it should be remembered that times were hard in the 30's and 40's. If he had money, he had to spend it to make a living for all the kids. He apparently never had a bank account. He was seen as a hard worker and seemed to always want to have more.

There was general agreement that he was hard to please and repeatedly said, "You can always do better." In relation to this, he was quite a disciplinarian and was viewed as having been excessive in this regard, to the point of being cruel and physically abusive.

He was musically inclined and they always had music in the home. One daughter said, "everyone sang around piano while he played." Another said he played beautifully." As a matter of fact, music was his special talent and he seemed to have special abilities in this area. He played the piano by ear, sometimes for the church. It seemed any and everything he did was done well and with music he had no limits, even in singing.

In his own way, he was a religious man. One daughter said it this way, "he claimed to be, but he used curse words real often, real bad ones." He attended the Methodist church, where he was a steward.

Most of the additional comments, which were contributed related to his temper, perfectionism, and abusive nature. However, there were some positive memories, too.

One daughter relates the following story:

"I remember when we lived at Petty, Texas, I was 7 or 8 and if someone came in to visit, he would want me to play the piano with him. I would cord on the left end and he did one hand on the other end."

A granddaughter related the following story:

"He loved banana pudding and coconut/pineapple cake with a seven-minute white frosting, which was a very moist cake.

I remember him scooping up the crumbs and digging a cellar in the remaining cake. He thought that roast and sweet potatoes were a special treat for lunch. Mother said that when cookies were being made, he ate half of the dough raw. She also said that he loved popcorn after supper. They would cook sorghum syrup down real low and make popcorn balls. They raised their own popcorn and sorghum cane. He had his own mill. A mule walked round and round to squeeze the juice out of the sorghum."

Another daughter also said he would go to his cousin's house at Cooper, Texas and be a single man, leaving his (first) wife at home caring for five kids.

A more positive statement, "David was an intellectual man, he should have been a lawyer. He knew the law and helped many people in his time."

Regarding his death, it was said, "He had a hard death. He had convulsions and an adult or two would have to hold him down until they wore down." He was suspected of having cancer.

Regarding the abuse, a daughter related the following story:

"He was on his best around outside people, our kinfolks and so forth. He took all his troubles and bitterness out on his kids. We were his slaves, his punching bags, someone to kick, use his belt on, or broom, mop, firewood, or whatever was near when the spell hit him. When I broke a bone, I got a beating before I got a doctor. If I was sick, I went to the field along with the rest. If I fainted, I got a cup of water in my face and sent back to the row."

An additional story was related by another daughter:

"When I was about 22 years old, I washed clothes and   made flour starch for my sisters. One sister came in and played in the house while I was churning and starting supper, after milking. This sister hadn't changed her school clothes and cried when I told her to change. Daddy got mad and beat me with a rope. I grabbed the rope and he wrapped it around my neck and chocked me. I had medical problems caused from the tight pressure of the rope on my neck."

She also reported additional medical problems which she said were related to his physical abuse.

There is no way to measure the extent of the emotional and psychological damage that was caused by the abuse. We now know that it has a way of playing itself out in many ways, often below one's level of awareness and often in a self-defeating manner. For example, people who were abused often become abusers themselves or attach themselves in relationships with abusive people.

In addition, we know that people who are abused often form a special kind of attachment to the abuser. In return, abusers often adopt an attitude of ownership toward their victims. Victims make the mistake of buying into this line of thinking and develop collusive alliances with the abuser, such as deciding to not talk openly of their treatment. This happens partly because shame, partly because they don't know it is abuse at the time and partly because a part of them believes they lost something valuable to the abuser and will never get it back. For example, victims may consciously or subconsciously believe the abuser took a portion of their childhood innocence. Also lost was a sense of safety and security in a world that was ultimately managed by a loving God. Another part believes they were partly responsible for the abuse. The victim feels they were to blame.

It seems that this shift in belief gives the abuser more power over their victims. It leads to the victim unknowingly protecting the abuser by keeping the whole thing a secret and feeling alone with their suffering. This power seems to persist and compete with the power of God, presenting obstacles to finding meaning in life. Beliefs such as this leave a lingering cloud of mistrust and skepticism that overshadows the most caring relationships and retards spiritual growth. These are abusive and harmful beliefs.

They are also not true which makes them lies. These lies must be revisited and challenged before trading them for more constructive beliefs about past events.

Remember, when we align ourselves with the purposes of heaven and act in the spirit of love, we are never alone. We have all of the natural forces working with us. Telling the truth about the past may be simple, as simple as a human hand, and it can be told gently, as gentle as a human touch.

When a single hand is aligned with the powers of heaven and earth, it can stand up to even the greatest lie, to the best kept secret, to the most stubborn habits, or the most firmly rooted family traditions. Whenever one parent is allowed to have absolute authority, the stage is set to have a family structured according to the ways of violence and neglect.

Such families will never know peace. Their members will always be restless or at war -- with others or within themselves. Therefore, if we align ourselves with God and let His spirit guide us, we will not go astray.

Finally, it may be helpful to consider our individual lives as like the individual leaves of a tree -- this family tree. No tree has leaves so foolish as to fight among themselves. There is no cause that justifies violence against another human being, except only in the last resort to protect yourself or family. Therefore, we are called to examine our behavior and conscience to identify those areas where we have tried to justify violence against others.

We are called to no longer dishonor the family by being known as one who is quick to anger. May all references to the "Haddock temper" cease to exist. Let us cultivate patience and tolerance, and let thoughtful wisdom characterize our lives. If we do become angry or confused, remember that it's not the emotion itself that brings dishonor. It is what we say and do while angry that creates problems.

Holding on to old anger also creates problems by keeping ourselves stuck in the past and creating illness. There is nothing wrong with anger if we have it and express it in a positive way. Anger held for a long time becomes resentment. These resentments held for a long time eat away at the body and contribute to diseases such as cancer and arthritis.

As we move through this section of family history, it becomes more apparent that past history is often safer to study because many of the personality details are lost. However, as we move into contemporary history these very traits are more available and contribute to our true knowledge of the people.

PART VI

Contemporary Haddocks

As we follow down the genealogical line, we come to Dave's son, Marvin. **William Marvin Haddock** married Miss Elsie Marie PIPKIN on November 5, 1932 in Hopkins County, Texas. They had eight children, seven of which survived (see Appendix X). All his children were born in Texas, although different counties. Elsie died at the early age of 37 after giving birth to our youngest brother. For more information regarding her ancestors, see appendices at the end on the Pipkin family. The facts about his life are listed below:

Focus: William Marvin Haddock (1910-1965)

When William Marvin Haddock was born on August 28, 1910, in Hopkins County, Texas, his father, William David, was 22 and his mother, Flora 'Trudy', was 19.

Marvin was married three times and had all his children with Elsie, his first wife: 5 sons and two daughters that survived They were all born in Texas. He died on September 5, 1965, in Commerce, Texas, at the age of 55, and was buried in Hopkins County, Texas.

America Enters World War I

When the United States declared war on Germany in 1917, William Marvin Haddock was living in Texas, but not of age to be drafted. Further, he worked most of his young life as a farmer and was exempted from military service.

Residences

From an unpublished book by Maredia Haddock Cunningham, entitled *Bittersweet Memories*, we know the existing occupational history of two generations and three families. "Our maternal and paternal grandparents were sharecroppers. Our parents followed in this tradition for many years. They worked and lived on other people's land for a share of the profit from the crops, mainly cotton, some corn and hi-gear. We often lived near one or both sets of grandparents."

We can take data from the Census and compare it to Maredia's book to get a more accurate picture of where Marvin moved his family over the years. While the Census puts Marvin's family living in three counties: Hunt, Hopkins, and Delta, Maredia adds that the family also lived in Lamar County.

Before marrying, in 1920, the census had him listed as single, son of head of house, living with his family of origin in Justice Precinct 4, Hopkins, Texas. By 1930, he the census had him living in Precinct 1, Hunt County, Texas. By 1932, he was married.

1935 • Rural, Hunt County, Texas

William Marvin Haddock lived in Delta County, Texas, on April 1, 1940.

"In 1945 we moved to the Paris, Texas area, along with our grandparents from both sides. We have some pictures taken at Brookston at Grandpa and Grandma Pipkin's house of a family gathering. We usually had family gatherings in the summer and at Christmas because some of mother's sisters lived in West Texas and that was the only time they could come home. Mother's older sister, Lynna (PIPKIN) Willis, always lived fairly close to us. She lived and reared her family in the Peerless and Pecan Gap areas."

Maredia added later, "In all, Odessa lived in 13 different places and I lived in 12 before we married and left home."

Occupation

Farmed, but rented as a sharecropper.[4] In 1954, he quit farming and moved to Commerce and was working as a janitor for the university when he died.

Education: Highest grade completed: High school, 1st year.

1st Marriage

William Marvin Haddock married Elsie Marie PIPKIN on November 5, 1932, in Hopkins County, Texas, when he was 22 years old. Both their families were already living in Texas and in neighboring communities at the time.

Birth of Children

His daughter Odessa Faye Haddock was born on October 31, 1935 and is still living. From the family Bible and written in Maredia's unpublished book: "I was born January 27, 1939 on a Friday at 2:20 A.M. in the hospital at Cooper, Texas. We lived at Klondike, Texas close to Papa Haddock and family

---

[4] This system became widespread in the southern states of the US after the Civil War, and it was in large part influenced by the end of slavery. There were both black and white sharecroppers well into the 1950s.

according to my sister, Odessa. She was the first born, October 31, 1935 on a Thursday at 1:00 A.M." … near the Commerce, Hunt County, Texas area.

Both of these daughters are still living and moved away from the Commerce area after they married, eventually retiring in the Ft. Worth area.

Marvin's first son, William Walter Haddock was born on November 28, 1940, and passed away that same day. They lived in the Miller Grove community, Hopkins County, Texas at that time. Maredia says, "We had moved near Miller Grove and we lived down the road to the south from Grandpa Grover Alton and Grandma Belva Mae Pipkin."

 His oldest living son Marvin Clifton was born in Hopkins County, Texas … "at our home west of Miller Grove on January 22, l943 on Friday at 11:20 P.M." according to Maredia. This would be on the Southwest end of Hopkins County and he settled in the area, currently living near the Northeast end of the county with land in the Klondike area.

Marvin's son Nolan Oneal was born on July 24, 1944, in Petty, Texas. From the family Bible and written in Maredia's unpublished book: "Oneal entered the world while we lived at Petty in the big house on July 24, 1944 on a Monday at 7:00 A.M." Oneal died in 2004 of a heart attack. He had several health problems, namely a rare form of arthritis, that contributed to the other health problems over time. He settled in the Commerce area, residing on the county line road between Hunt and Delta County, near Klondike, at the time of his death.

Nolan Oneal Haddock - 1944–2004

His son Billy Dan was born on August 13, 1948, in the Branom Community, Hopkins County, Texas and is still living. He moved away in his mid-thirties and now resides in the College Station, Texas area.

His son William Alton was born on April 17, 1950, in Commerce, Texas and is still living in the area.

His son Gary David Haddock was born on May 29, 1953, in Commerce, Texas and is still living. He settled in the East Texas area, near Jacksonville.

 Marvin's wife Elsie Marie passed away on May 29, 1953 after giving birth to Gary David, in Commerce, Texas, at the age of 37. They had been married 20 years. Cause of death: Post-partum hemorrhaging.

Second Marriage

William Marvin Haddock moved the family into Commerce after buying a two-story house on Lee Street from Lemuel Deloss Parsons, a chemistry professor at the college. The house was just a half block from campus. He married Vay Simpson Gillian in 1956 when he was 46 years old. She had never been married and they had no children together. They divorced after a few years' marriage.

Iller LeVay GILLIAN - 1914–2012

Third Marriage

William Marvin married Hazel Gatha Quinn in June 1962 in Commerce, Texas, when he was 51 years old. They lived together until his death in 1965.

Hazel Gatha Quinn - 1911–2003

Death

William Marvin Haddock died of cancer on September 5, 1965, in Commerce, Texas, when he was 55 years old and is buried with Elsie Marie, William Walter and Oneal in Mt. Zion Cemetery, Branom community Hopkins County, Texas. (See Appendix X)

Spotlight on Elsie Marie PIPKIN Haddock

Our immediate family spent 37 years talking very little about our mother, Elsie. Consequently, many of her younger children knew very little about her because they were so young and grief stricken when she died. This section focuses on her, first, so that all who follow may get a glimpse of the "special" nature of the person we called 'mother.'

Most agree the features that stood out about Elsie were her soft blue eyes, her blonde hair and her fair complexion. Her favorite colors were blue and pink. A pink chiffon dress and a medium blue suit, which she made herself, were among her favorite clothes.

The words that were most often used to describe Elsie's personality were: kind and gentle, perhaps gentle as a lamb. She was also described as "easy-going and real tender-hearted," especially toward animals. She always liked to pet the dogs, cats and even cows and horses. In addition, she kept chickens. Her disposition and kindness always stood out. She was very patient and seldom fussy. She tended to be quiet, had a good sense of humor and smiled a lot. She was a good mother, wife, sister and friend.

Elsie apparently enjoyed eating. Consequently, she was remembered for having been a good cook. Among the favorites from her kitchen that were mentioned were biscuits, yeast rolls, syrup cake, and tea cookies. She also did a lot of canning, as was the custom of that time, and always had lots of canned food from the garden. She was known for growing a good garden that included vegetables and flowers, such as zinnias, marigolds, sweet Williams, petunias, bachelor buttons, and sweet peas. She also had a lot of houseplants.

She married when she was 16 and had to work in the fields, like many farm-oriented families did in those days. She showed an early talent at helping with the younger children. She seemed to have a knack of getting them to do what she wanted. In addition, she showed a lot of common sense in raising her own children. If she and her husband, Marvin, had trouble, she wouldn't fuss back at him. She would go someplace and cry. Although not known to have a nickname, apparently, Marvin had a pet name for her, or teased her in some way that made her blush.

Elsie never held a public job. She spent what Marvin gave her, even if the family worked together in the cotton fields. They decided together how the money would be spent. She learned to be a good manager and could make money go a long way. Many times, the family had only a limited amount of food or clothes, but they never went hungry or dirty. She embroidered, quilted some and made most of our clothes to assist in this effort. I even remember an old blue and red short set she probably made from flour sack material, which was another custom of the times.

Elsie was religious all her life. She was saved at an early age and much of her dating with daddy was centered around church services. Although they didn't travel much, she enjoyed visiting her parents, relatives, and their few close friends.

Sister, Adaline shared a memory about Elsie when they were growing up. Adaline was sitting across from Elsie at the table, watching her eat and remembered thinking to herself how Elsie enjoyed eating. Another sister, Ester, shared another childhood memory. When Elsie was about 13, she had to go into the pasture to get the cows. Along the way, she found a dead snake. So, she thought it would be funny to get her sister, Lynna, to hold her hands out with her eyes closed and give her the snake. When she did, it scared Lynna badly. Elsie was so sorry she did it, but she never thought it would scare Lynna that badly. Elsie's daughter, Maredia, fondly remembers mother waiting in her rocking chair near the front door for the kids to get off the school bus and share their day with her. Sometimes they would have cookies and sometimes just a piece of cornbread. It seems she left many fond memories in the lives of those she touched.

From the Pipkin family, Elsie probably inherited a tendency toward skin cancer due to their fair complexion. From the Fleenor family she may have inherited a predisposition toward diabetes and high blood pressure. She developed asthma the last couple of years of her life and couldn't always breathe when she would first lay down at night (see back for more information on the Fleenor and Pipkin families).

Elsie died on May 29, 1953 around 5:30 pm after giving birth to Gary David, her eighth child (as mentioned William Walter died soon after birth). Apparently, her uterus collapsed during that last childbirth and she bled to death. It seemed such a senseless death. The doctor and nurses in the small clinic where she was located were not equipped to perform a blood transfusion or surgery.

Her sister, Ava, shares the following account of the impact of mother's death on her life:

"I remember the morning we got the call she had died. I just could not believe it had happened. Up to that time I had never been saved. After that happened, the Lord spoke to me and made me realize that this could happen to any one of us and that we needed to be prepared to die. For a long time, it was hard for me to accept what happened to her. But, later, I realized that God has a plan for all of us. We just never know when or how."

This tragic incident was talked about very little in the family for many years. It could be simply viewed through a child's eyes that Elsie was a victim of circumstances. A victim of **place**: living in a rural area near a small town with few medical services. A victim of **time**: 1953 offered few of the medical procedures and technology, including birth control methods, we now have. A victim of **person**(s): depending upon point of view, it could be argued that her inconsiderate husband, who conceived the baby...or...the irresponsible doctor, who delivered the baby...or...the innocent baby, himself...any one of these persons could be blamed for her death.

However, instead of guilt, shame, and disadvantage, I now choose to honor the role of all people and circumstances in this event and look toward the advantages. Much of my life I have worked at bringing honor to myself and the family name in general. But my daughter, Kristi, taught me an important lesson. True honor comes from humbly allowing God to work through our lives in difficult situations.

Only a spiritual viewpoint offers this honor. If we choose to see this and other tragic events as designed by God for our spiritual growth and development, then we must conclude that God honored Elsie beyond our comprehension. If this is so, then we have no choice other than to love and honor all persons involved. Only by shifting our views regarding Elsie's death, can we prepare to fully receive God's gifts for us.

It has been said that Elsie loved her flower garden. Her widowed husband, Marvin often said, "flowers are for the living." It could be assumed this was a statement regarding the importance of expressing one's feelings toward loved ones with flowers on special occasions. In addition, it could be addressing the fact that funerals and the customary flowers are all part of the rituals for the living to assist in grieving our losses. In any case, I am often reminded of flowers when thinking of Elsie. For example, someone else said (when speaking of Elsie's death), "when God picks a flower, He picks the best one." The complexities of love and loss are often represented in the symbolic language of flowers. No one is ever prepared for the loss of a loved one. However, people who do the work of grief do begin to heal with time and learn that even the worst losses can burst into bloom. I believe there comes a time in life when we must all bloom where we are planted. There comes, at a proper time in the life cycle, a bloom, regardless of height, growth, soil conditions, nutrients, or trauma to the plant. These all affect the height of the plant and quality of the bloom, but the bloom comes anyway. It is a life force that will manifest itself.

Whether these stories, meanings or images reflect the true picture of Elsie is not important. What is important is how we use these associations to affect the ways in which we live our lives. A flower which does not open cannot receive what is needed to contribute to its continuing growth and life. It seems we must be taught to open up more and learn from each other. Flowers can bloom in her name through the lives of all her descendants who choose to strive to become their "higher selves" and dedicate their lives to love, peace and gentleness.

More on **William Marvin Haddock**

This next step down the genealogical line represents another ancestor who made a career change in the family while still relatively young, moving from the farm after Elsie's death and becoming a blue-collar worker.

It is not known if he had a nickname. Like his father, Dave, he went by his middle name, Marvin, even though his name was William Marvin. The tradition of going by the middle name continues into the next generation of Haddocks as well.

There were several features that stand out about Marvin Haddock. Most notable were his pride and his love for his family. He had several noticeable physical features: his high cheek bones, dark wavy hair with receding hair line on the front and bald spot at the back, his blue eyes and glasses, well-developed arm muscles, large rough hands, broad shoulders and smile. It was also noted that he had a certain look he would get when in deep thought.

Regarding his manner of dress, he preferred blue in a suit for church and special occasions, slacks and a dress shirt for casual dress and seemed to favor wearing khaki clothes for work. He usually wore a felt hat in the winter and mostly wore shoes, but also liked a good pair of boots. He always dressed neat and was always clean.

He traveled very little. He would drive around on Sunday afternoon with the family to nearby towns. He traveled most to visit children or relatives, such as to North Carolina to see son, Clifton and to Georgia to see daughter, Maredia and Vernon, Texas about three times to see Elsie's sister, Ester and daughter, Odessa when she lived there. Marvin didn't visit friends that often, but he would visit people he worked with about once a month. They would usually get together and play dominoes with three or four couples.

He had a horse most of the time, even when he lived in town. Having a horse was his one hobby he afforded himself. He usually had a dog. He also had previously raised game chickens and fought the roosters, but without metal spurs and did not fight them to the point of death.

Sometimes, he liked to pick at people and tease. He would tell of playing practical jokes quite often, but didn't play them much at home. When the boys were very young, he would take out his dentures and scare the younger kids. He seemed to laugh often, especially during his later years when amusing things happened. Overall, Marvin was not seen as being light-hearted. Most children saw him as being heavy hearted. There were times when he missed his deceased wife, Elsie, a lot and his sadness was often seen and felt by his children. When younger, he drank alcohol some. His sister shared some about his drinking as a young adult. It seems he went through the usual pattern of hiding his early experimenting from his father and had some experiences of excessive use while he was learning to drink. She tells one story of how she helped him get home and put to bed without calling attention of

Dave, their father. Marvin seldom drank when he was older. He started back later in life at the suggestion of his doctor to help him relax and it was usually at the end of the day when he would have one or two beers.

It was generally agreed that he had common sense. He used to say, "What are you going to do without me" referring to what seemed to him as a general lack of common sense and ability to do things well that many parents notice in their children.

There was general agreement that he was a good manager. Due to the financial limitations of the family, we never seemed to have enough money. Therefore, considering his low income and the size of family, he probably would qualify as an excellent manager. This is another example of necessity being the mother of invention. He became a good manager out of necessity. It should be noted that he was considered a generous man when he had money, but that wasn't very often. He was very careful how he spent money. He seemed to enjoy growing a garden, even though it was also out of necessity, and had flowers in it as well. He also raised chickens for the meat and eggs. He occasionally had a cow for the milk. He never seemed to have enough money and would buy the cheaper or less expensive kinds of food, clothes, and so forth.

He attended church with his family and was a member of the Methodist church. He apparently never really discussed religion with his children though. He read the Bible some at night. Marvin liked church music, piano music and loved to sing. He played some pieces on the piano from memory and played the French harp by ear.

Marvin had many special talents and abilities. He could do things with his hands well, such as mechanical work, carpentry, and electrical work. He could do a little of everything and do a fair job of it, from cooking and housework to working on a car and building a barn. He worked for other people to earn extra income for his family. One son attributes his interest in developing a variety of skills to Marvin by saying, "I guess that's where I got to be a jack of all trades and master of none". He was also considered to be good with horses and in raising his children.

There were mixed opinions regarding his being a perfectionist. It was agreed that he liked things in place, people to be on time, and things done right. He emphasized that he wanted it to be right. Related to the perfectionism, there were also mixed opinions regarding Marvin being hard to please. Most opinions were qualified by statements such as, "not if you did what he expected" and "as long as you did what you said you would."

He was described as not bossy. One son put it in proper perspective by saying he was "...the boss, but not bossy". Another described him as a "mild mannered boss." It was also agreed that he was firm and consistent. His form of discipline was primarily to whip with a belt. In the earlier days, he had one of those notorious razor straps. He would often wait until he was angry and would get excessive with his discipline. There is a fine line between being excessive and abusive. Whether it was excessive or abusive, the experiences were memorable for all children and often date back to early childhood.

For example, one of my earliest memories was just a fragment that lingered in my mind for many years:

"I remember when I was very young that a rooster attacked my little brother. I became angry and cursed. My dad whipped me with a board."

Since I remembered little details, a creative approach to dealing with this was used by working it into a fairy tale. The story is shown in the following paragraphs.

"Once upon a time...there were two brothers, ages 3 and 1, who lived in a small rural kingdom inhabited by giants. There were giant cows, giant horses, giant chickens, and a giant rooster who would lie await on the pathway for a solitary brother and attack. For you see, the rooster was larger, meaner, and much more aggressive than a single brother -- but the rooster would not attack two brothers at once. Then one day, the older of the two brothers was working on a fence with the father giant. The younger brother was walking along the pathway alone and was attacked by the giant rooster.

The older brother seemed too far away to come to younger brother's aid, but he did express his anger at the rooster -- "That damn rooster!" Then the father giant picked up a board and whipped the older brother for cursing. Two attacks took place that day....

However, there was a spiritual dimension of this event that went almost unnoticed. After the beating, there was a spiritual struggle for the little child to rise above the occasion, claim a sense of identity as a precious child of God and run to his brother's aid. For what seemed like an instant in eternal measurements ended up being over 30 years before the spiritual response was realized. During this time, the little child was frozen by fear of rejection by the father giant, often paralyzed each time he felt angry emotions, and experienced the kingdom as a hostile and threatening place.

Many years have passed since this event. The mother giant died a year or two after the attack. Several years later, the father giant also died. And now both brothers are giants, themselves. The older brother tried to be the family hero and spent a lot of time saving family members and other people by fighting giants, but was many times paralyzed by his own anger. The younger brother acted like the family clown and continues to entertain people with his humor and wit, but feels very lonely at times.

After many years, the spiritual response has now been released. The older brother previews the old scene and pictures himself looking at little brother, running to him and rescuing him. The father giant is no longer enraged, but stunned and in awe as he observes the older brother taking a beating, running to rescue the little brother and making a victorious sound that glorifies God. - The End.

Creative writing, such as this, is a very useful way to bring healing to old hurts and memories. It assists in releasing emotions held for years and helps uncover additional dimensions of old memories. We remember facts and events often because strong emotions are connected to them.

Dreams are another way to gather information about ourselves in relation to the past, present and future. They were spoken of often in the Old Testament. A personal example occurred on January 18, 1990. I had a dream that dates earlier than any actual memory:

> I dreamed that William and I were very little. I was about 3 and he was about 1. We were happy, smiling and excited about going to see Daddy at work out at the blacksmith shop. We left the chicken house holding hands and carrying 2 pullet eggs (1 each) to show Daddy. He was working in the shop grinding on something metal (like a plow) on some kind of grinder that had to be pumped by foot. As we approached Daddy, we told him we missed him and we had just come to visit. We each hugged him as he leaned down for us. I distinctly remember the feel of his whiskers on my face. William's little boy smile was very animated and full of expression. This expression seemed very real and familiar. We showed Daddy the eggs and then he disappeared inside the shop. While we were waiting for him we entertained each other by holding the eggs close to each other's eyes and looking at them closely and smiling. The dream ended while the grinder slowly came to a halt.

This was a pure, innocent dream that left a distinct feeling of Daddy's whiskers on my face even after I awakened. I have dreamed often of Daddy through the years and we often have very good conversations. These dreams have become some of my fondest memories that are often difficult to separate from actual memories lingering in my mind of the past, except that I have recorded these dreams in a journal.

Another very different experience I remember illustrates how Marvin's character and abilities were appreciated by his friends and co-workers. I was in the library at East Texas State University (now Texas A&M-Commerce) in the Fall of 1976 and Dr. John Burke, then Library Science Department Head, related the following story to me: He said that since my dad's death eleven years earlier, the men who have painted the library have painted around an inscription Marvin made near the breaker box in the mechanical room. It simply stated, "W.M. Haddock, 1959". This was the date they moved into the new library where he worked until his death. Dr. Burke said he wanted to tell me this story to illustrate how much Marvin was respected and liked by people in his community.

Like the alpha wolf in a pack, Marvin loved his family with all his heart and protected them. Wolves are known for protecting children. They are very good with children. He did what he could and what he had to do to keep us together, feed us, clothe us and keep us in school. He was constantly giving of himself to meet our needs. His children felt that protection and faithfulness. As one son stated, "He was a good man, a strong man and sometimes a hard man. But he loved us all and was there for us until the end. I would be happy just to be his equal." In response to his being there for us, we loved him. This is simply stated by one child, "I loved and admired him very much."

In considering the way Marvin parented and looked after us, I have many times stated that he was a hard act to follow, meaning he left a very good model of loyalty and faithfulness toward family and children. I used this model for years in my own parenting. The following dream expands on this subject more:

> On April 17, 1988 I dreamed about Daddy, who was sitting among us at a family reunion and smiling. I spoke to him of my desire to not feel like I had to be responsible for anyone else but me. I talked to him about his model of responsibility with us kids and he said not to try to duplicate his life, but to live our own. In the dream, he said he did what he did because we (kids) were all he had. This brought thoughts of how his love for us bonded us kids. Finally, he said that both he and mother were continuously concerned about our (kids) welfare even now, since they died.

I have come to understand more about this in my adult life. A lot of Marvin's motivations were out of a sense of guilt and grief over Elsie's death. I knew of his sadness, but didn't connect the grief to guilt until I was older. Marvin left many beliefs and sayings echoing in the minds of his children. One of them I remember was, "five minutes of pleasure can bring a lifetime of regret". I used to think this was meant to be a father's instruction to a child to emphasize the importance of keeping your sexual urges within proper boundaries. Now, I see this as indicating his own regrets and guilt for having participated in a brief act that contributed to Elsie's death. This is especially applicable in light of information that suggests that Elsie's problems with childbirth were identified much earlier with the birth of a stillborn child. Reportedly, they were warned then that next time it would be her and not the child who would not make it through the birth.

Another piece of information connects to this. I remember as a child that remarks were made concerning mother's death by bleeding. It was often stated, "she was a bleeder". In my child-like mind, I thought she was a hemophiliac or free bleeder. This was not the case. This remark referred to her problems with childbirth. Her uterus had a tendency to pull away from the walls of the womb and cause bleeding. She was only a bleeder during childbirth. Now the guilt and sense of commitment to the surviving children becomes more apparent.

Due to Marvin's natural loyalty and lingering guilt, an excessive sense of commitment to the children got put in motion. Sometimes, when this happens, it elevates children to a position of importance over one's own needs. When carried to an extreme, it elevates children to a position of being treated like God and they feel Godlike. When parents worship children or children worship parents, it empowers them (the one being worshipped) rather than God or your own self to decide on things. It's a commitment that feels like a need to penalize or do penitence. There is a spirit of debt or obligation incurred, which tends to overshadow the spirit of love. You can't serve two masters. In a committed relationship, it works better if you state preferences and then align yourself with your Higher self. Any type of excessive commitment in relationships contributes to self-neglect and allows people -- spouses, kids, or friends to bleed you dry.

People tend to speak from different levels of truth. We are often unaware that other people speak from truths different from ours and tend to label those differences as "untruths" or lies. When a person is operating from a particular level of truth, that level is "true" for him or her. People often go for years holding a certain truth until circumstances bring about a new way of thinking about things that contribute to a new truth. As we move to higher levels of truth, each new level is almost always the opposite of the previous one. Although this gives the appearance of inconsistency, it represents a growth in awareness.

For example, on one level, Marvin was a good man, a hard act to follow. On another level, a logical adult level, it was really a bad thing for daddy to make love to mother and have her die. Even though I believe all the children were conceived in the spirit of genuine and everlasting love, it seems frivolous and irresponsible for both parents to conceive additional children after they were warned of the possible complications. It could be easy for a child to witness this and decide to never be irresponsible on that or any level. On another level, we can imagine daddy's pain and anger at himself because he knew the good and the bad of this situation. Holding that much anger can cause you not to trust yourself and to act out that pain occasionally. Imagine mother's pain of knowing she might not survive the pregnancy to see her children grow. On another, higher level of truth, there is simply no one to blame. They were all innocent participants in God's plan. Although we do not completely understand the "whys" about this, let us walk in these truths, honor God's plan and hold an even higher truth: eternal love conquers death.

There is no doubt that Marvin carried on the affairs of being a good parent. I imagine this was often done by the strength of his will and character, in addition to being motivated by guilt. The helmet of this "William" was demonstrated by a protective nature that was also hard at times. And now, since he has gone from this life, I can only hope and pray that his helmet has been transformed into something softer, like a halo.

It has been said that any time someone's life is cut short in the earth, there is a response from both heaven and earth that attempts to complete things that life represented. For example, the life and untimely death of Jesus triggered a response that invited each one of us to complete the life that the crucifixion interrupted. Simply stated, we are called to complete a life of service to others through Jesus' death and resurrection. Similarly, we are called to complete the lives cut short in our family. In mother's life and death, we are called to live and flower in the spirit of gentleness. With daddy's life and death, we are called to continue living with loyalty and faithfulness to God, self, family and others. When we move forward with love and courage, then a sense of completion will be felt. By living in this manner, no one would have died in vain.

It was believed by Native Americans that if someone dies without having anybody to remember him and cry for him, then the mourning dove remembers and mourns for him. Therefore, if you remember somebody you loved that died, then the mourning dove would not have to mourn for them. So, when you hear the mourning dove, remember Elsie, Marvin and all other relatives who have gone before us and the dove won't sound so lonesome. Also, remember the sacrifice that Christ made for you. This will also help us remember that we are never really alone.

Generational Gaps

The characteristics of the wolf, my favorite animal, can be instructive to us in another way besides the way Marvin parented his children. The wolf can show us how to remember the best examples of both Elsie and Marvin's lives. The wolf captures the essence of wanting to demonstrate the gentle nature of a lamb, to be loving and caring like Elsie. It is also loyal and protective, like Marvin, and has pretty sharp fangs and claws to use in self-defense, if it came to it. The wolf instructs us to love the whole self, even the part that makes a biting remark every once in a while. Failure to love the whole self brings about divided loyalties. There is no reason to have divided loyalties between Elsie and Marvin or within yourself.

Embrace that part of you that has been even slightly abusive. There's a reason for abuse, inconsideration and even crankiness. It's part of human nature and by allowing it and owning up to it, you can watch it and keep it in balance. Remember, gentleness gets angry too. Therefore, it is helpful to see any rough feeling as part of human nature and the wolf can direct us to making a fierce alignment with our Higher selves. This alignment contributes to the ability to demonstrate strength without having any attack in it. We can also develop the ability to show a very strong presence without the need for hurtful words or actions.

Since Marvin's death, the surviving children have gone on in life, often by sheer will and determination. At the time this is being updated, the oldest daughter, Odessa, is widowed and lives in Joshua, Texas where she is retired as a teacher's aide. In recent years, she has struggled with her husband's and daughter's death, her own cancer and the related treatment, the problems of being a surviving parent whose son divorced, and aging. However, she carries on, manages daily living and maintains a positive example of strength for the family.

Sister, Maredia, is married and lives in Arlington, Texas where she has retired as a teacher. She continues to be a major source of faith and support by serving as a "mother figure" for the extended family.

Oldest brother, Clifton, continues the family tradition of living with the land by fighting to survive as a semi-retired rancher. He lives near Dyke, Texas and can usually be found somewhere near the places he loves so much, outside with nature.

Brother, Oneal died in 2004 and was retired with the postal service to the position as postmaster in Commerce, Texas.

I retired as a counselor in College Station, Texas and studied in college on and off until I was over forty.

Brother, William, lives in Campbell, Texas and has had the most varied occupational history by "stubbornly" trying his hand as truck driver, carpenter, railroad brakeman, businessman, and facilities manager at Texas A&M-Commerce.

Youngest brother, Gary David, lives near Tyler and has a long work history with several telephone companies as an engineer.

At this point, the lineage of Haddocks comes to a pause. Hank Devin Haddock, oldest son of Marvin Clifton Haddock was killed in an automobile accident without any descendants of his own. Clifton's next son, Jake Texas Haddock has not married at the time of this publication. Wesley Haddock, son of Nolan Oneal Haddock, married and has two daughters. The rest of the boys had daughters. Therefore, the pause may result in the elimination of this particular surname which has been traced.

These surviving children serve as examples of the helmet of resolution mentioned earlier in relation to the "Williams" of the Haddock family. Our determination has been reflected in other ways than those mentioned in the above paragraph. It is also seen in our stubborn insistence to parent our children, each other and even our spouses in some cases. It is also seen in our stubborn adherence to seeing our way (or opinion) as the right way or only way. This is often problematic when unwanted or uninvited because it gets in the way of enjoying these very important relationships with family and friends. The time has come to move from a "survivor" status. We can use the Haddock sense of determination to move forward in the family history by developing skills to enjoy a sense of abundance and happiness. This may be the most importance inheritance we can leave future generations.

It is well known that many problems in families get handed down from one generation to another. Therefore, this look back into the family history may have offered some insights into the origin of current problems in the lives of contemporary Haddocks and their descendants. I hope this genealogical search will serve as a bridge between any relatives cut off by past events and serve as the means for opening doors that may have been closed. Discussions about deceased ancestors can help the family heal old wounds in indirect ways. I know because it has helped me in making contact with relatives so often neglected by a busy schedule, geographic distances, generation gaps and old feuds from the past.

I encourage all interested descendants of the Haddock family to continue genealogical research and add additional chapters and family charts. There are bits and pieces of information that are left blank in the following appendices.

In addition, you will find some blank family data forms. These are provided to continue working on your family history. In this way, you can personalize your history and preserve it for future generations.

Note:

Historical information in the section on Elsie and Marvin came from the relatives mentioned or alluded to above as the result of a written family survey. Text and editorial comment were prepared by son, Billy Dan Haddock.

Postscript:

The main body of the poem on the following page was written shortly after Marvin's death. The original poem ended with the angels also asking "why?". The last four lines were recently added, which I think is symbolic of a sense of completion I feel as the result of this search. This is offered up for anyone who has loved and lost….

Billy D. Haddock

Upon his death

Why must he on earth be born,

When people live in ungodly scorn?

Why does God let him grow,

Where all these evils he will know?

And as this man lives his life,

Why must it be so full of strife?

Soon a woman comes along,

And before he knew, she did him wrong.

Why must he look with worried eyes

as every hope he had merely dies?

Why must problems overwhelm him

To make his outlook on life grow dim?

He toils all day and part of night,

Oh, God! Will life ever be right?

His fight is strong but his body weak,

Why must life be so bleak?

Generational Gaps

Then he asks with dying breath

Why must life be full of death?

A soul then rises to the sky,

Says the angels, "Here's why..."

You were placed on Mother Earth to live and die,

To overcome disadvantage and the problems of "why!",

To claim a heartfelt strength which flows from above

And shatter death's illusion with eternal love.

- Billy D. Haddock -

References

Andrews, C. M. (1934). *The Colonial Period of American History.* Yale University Press.

Booth, G. (1916). *Bury St. Edmunds, St. James Parish Registers, Marriages 1562-1800.* Woodbridge, England.

Brown, A. (1898). *The First Republic in America.* Boston: Houghton, Mifflin & Co.

Camden, W. (1551-1623). In *Elizabethan historian.*

Crook, B. (n.d.). *http://www.historyofparliamentonline.org/volume/1660-1690/member/haddock-sir-richard-1629-1715.* Retrieved from http://www.historyofparliamentonline.org.

EDWARD MAUNDE THOMPSON, E. (24 March, 1881). *Correspondence of the family of Haddock, 1657-1719.* NICHOLS AND SONS.

Goldfield, D. (2005). *NCPedia.* Retrieved from Early Settlement: http://www.ncpedia.org/history/colonial/early-settlement?page=7

Haddock, H. R. (1976). *Legends of the Haddock Family.*

Haddock, H. R. (undated). *Legends of the Haddock Family.* Grants Pass: Oregon.

Haddock, J. N. (1964). *The Haddock family of Essex, England, Pitt County, North Carolina, and Georgia, USA.* Atlanta, Georgia.

http://docs.gravesham.gov.uk/WebDocs/Environment%20and%20Planning/Conservation_Areas/Milton_Place_Appraisal.pdf). (n.d.).

http://docs.gravesham.gov.uk/WebDocs/Environment%20and%20Planning/Conservation_Areas/Milton_Place_Appraisal.pdf). (n.d.).

http://en,wikipaedia.org/wiki/Richard_Haddock. (n.d.).

http://en,wikipaedia.org/wiki/Richard_Haddock, n.d. (n.d.).

http://forebears.io/surnames/haddock. (n.d.).

http://www.emmigration.info/english-immigration-to-america.htm. (n.d.).

https://en.wikipedia.org/wiki/Mile_End. (n.d.). Retrieved from https://en.wikipedia.org.

https://en.wikipedia.org/wiki/Panic_of_1837. (n.d.). Retrieved from https://en.wikipedia.org.

https://www.history.org/history/teaching/tchcrsta.cfm. (n.d.). Retrieved from https://www.history.org.

Loose Leaves of the History of Lamar County. (1921, July 12). Paris, Texas: The Paris News.

Maryland, S. o. (1679-1783). *Settlers of Maryland, .*

Peter the Great. (n.d.). Retrieved from Wikipedia, the free encyclopedia). .

Rodger, N. (1997). *The Safeguard of the Sea.* London: Norton & Co.

She reported that at least two were legible: Ezra Haddock and his wife, Ida Earlhttp://www.seacoastnh.com/History/As-I-Please/did-haddocks-settle-maine-in-1610/). (n.d.). Retrieved from www.seacoastnh.com.

The reliquary and illustrated archaeologist. (1895). London: Bemrose and Sons.

Warwicker, M. E. (1973). *A tradition of service: A study of the Haddock family.* Essex, England.

Weir, E. (1909). *DIARY OF AN 1858 WAGON TRAIN JOURNEY.* Retrieved from Pope County Historical Association: http://www.argenweb.net/pope/wagon.html

Wesley Historical Society. (n.d.).

Wesley, J. (Vol. IV, p. 426). John Wesley's Journal.

www.wikepedia.org/millercounty. (n.d.). Retrieved from www.wikepedia.org.

Appendix I - Sir Richard Haddock, Admiral

Relation to author: 8th great grandfather

Facts

Age 0 — Birth

May 1629 • Wapping, Middlesex, England

Parish History All Hallows Barking: Timeline 675 - founded; oldest church in London 1650 - gunpowder explosion destroyed church tower 1658 - church tower rebuilt 1940s - bombed during London Blitz, later restored

Birth *(Alternate)*

1629 • 1671374, Middlesex, England

Age 1 — Birth of Brother Lt. Joseph Haddock**(1631–1696)**

1631 • Leigh On, Essex, England

Age 1 — Birth of Sister Jane Jessica Haddock**(1631–)**

1631 • Leigh, Essex, England

Age 3 — Birth of Brother Andrew Haddock**(1633–)**

1633 • Leigh On Sea, Essex, , England

Age 5 — Birth of Sister Sarah Haddock**(1635–)**

1635 • London, London, England

Age 7 — Birth of Brother William Haddock**(1637–1672)**

23 Apr 1637 • St. Giles Cripplegate, London, London, England

Age 10 — Birth of Brother Ellis Haddock**(1639–)**

Nov 05, 1639 • London, London, England

Age 11 — Birth of Brother Nicholas Haddock**(1640–)**

Nov 25, 1640 • Stepney, London, England

Age 13 — Birth of Sister Maria Haddock**(1643–)**

Abt. 1643

Age 17 — Birth of Brother John Haddock**(1647–)**

Mar 19, 1647 • Cripplegate, London, England

Age 18 — Marriage

13 Feb 1648 • Collegiate Church of St Katherine by the Tower, London, England

First wife - died 1670

Elizabeth "Lydia" Wilkinson

(1630–1670)

Age 21 — Birth of Daughter Jeane Haddock**(1650–)**

Nov 1650 • London, London, England

Age 23 — Birth of Daughter Elizabeth Haddock**(1653–1728)**

1653 • All Hallows Barking, London, England

Age 23 — Birth of Son John I Haddock**(1653–1728)**

30 Mar 1653 • London, Middlesex, England

Age 26 — Birth of Son Richard Haddock**(1655–1751)**

Nov 22, 1655 • London, London, England

Age 28 — Excerpt from letter to his father

30 May 1657 • england

"Sir, my wife desires yo u please, at yo r arrivall at Ven% to buy for her a foiled stone of the measure I conseave was given by her sisters to Brother Andrew at Leighas alsoe a pott ketle and 2 stue panns, one lesser than the other; as alsoe a jarr .."

Age 28 — Employment

1657

Already a Captain in command of the Dragon frigate.

Age 37 — Employment

1666 • england

Captain of the Portland

Age 38 — Death of Father CAPT. WILLIAM Haddock**(1607–1667)**

22 Sep 1667 • Leigh-on-the Sea, Essex, England-St Clement Churchyard Cem.

Age 38 — Employment

1667 • england

1667-71 - engaged in trading to the Mediterranean.

Age 40 — Birth of Daughter <u>Lydia Haddock</u>**(1670–1732)**

Abt. 1670 • England

Age 41 — Death of Wife <u>Elizabeth "Lydia" Wilkinson</u>**(1630–1670)**

1670 • London, London, , England

Age 42 — Marriage

27 Jul 1671 • St Christopher le Stocks, London, England

First wife - died 1670. He was listed as a widower, age 40 & she is listed at a spinster at age 20. Marriage with consent of her governors & relations. Place St.Botolph, Bishopsgate.

<u>Elizabeth Betty Hurleston</u>

(1650–1709)

Age 42 — Birth of Daughter <u>Martha Haddock</u>**(1672–1722)**

1672 • London, London, England

Age 42 — Death of Brother <u>William Haddock</u>**(1637–1672)**

08 Apr 1672 • London, London, England

Age 43 — Employment

Bet. 1672–1714 • england

Comptroller of His Majesties Navy (1689), Navy Commissioner (1672, First Commissioner of Victualing Yard (1683), & Joint Commander-in-Chief of the Fleet (1714)

Age 43 — Birth of Son <u>Richard HADDOCK Capt</u>**(1673–1751)**

1673 • All Hallows Barking, London, , England

Age 51 — Birth of Son <u>William Haddock Sr.</u>**(1681–)**

1681 • London, Middlesex, England

Age 56 — Birth of Son <u>Admiral Nicholas Haddock</u>**(1685–1746)**

8 November 1685 • London, Middlesex, England

Age 58 — Death of Mother <u>Mary Anna Goodlad</u> **(1602–1688)**

06 Jan 1688 • Leigh On Sea, Essex, England

Age 67 — Death of Brother <u>Lt. Joseph Haddock</u>**(1631–1696)**

1696 • London, London, England

Age 71 — Employment

1700's • england

Comptroller of His Majesties Navy

Age 79 — Death of Wife <u>Elizabeth Betty Hurleston</u>**(1650–1709)**

Feb 26, 1709 • All Hallows Barking, London, England

Age 81 — Residence

1710 • Portsoken, England

Portsoken, England Borough or County: City of London

Age 85 — Trinity House Membership

1714 • Leigh On Sea, Essex, , England

Richard1453, John (his son), Capt Richard1660, Capt Wm1667, SirRichard1714, AdmNicholas1746, WmGoodland1639, Capt.RichardGoodland1693grant of a Royal Charter by Henry VIII in 1514. Charter granted by Henry VIII in 1514

Age 85 — Burial

15 Jan 1715-1716 • Leigh-on-Sea, Essex, England

Age 85 — Death

26 Jan 1715 • All Hallows Barking, London, Middlesex, England

Age at Death: 85

Residence

1715 • London

Looks like probate records

Inspiration for Book

1940's • Belgium

His story coincides with Herge's creation of the fictional Captain Haddock's flamboyant ancesteor Sr. Francis Haddock in 'The Secret of the Unicorn.' Popular in the '40's and made in to a movie. Comic book format.

Appendix II - John I Haddock

Relation to author: 7th great grandfather

Facts

Age 0 — Birth

30 Mar 1653 • London, Middlesex, England

Birth *(Alternate)*

Mar 30, 1653 • London, Greater London, England

Baptism

30 Mar 1653 • St Bartholomew by the Exchange, London, England

this is William's baptism, son of John I, not John I. Must have been done by proxy, since they lived in Maryland.

Age 2 — Birth of Brother <u>Richard Haddock</u>**(1655–1751)**

Nov 22, 1655 • London, London, England

Age 16 — Birth of Sister <u>Lydia Haddock</u>**(1670–1732)**

Abt. 1670 • England

Age 17 — Death of Mother <u>Elizabeth "Lydia" Wilkinson</u>**(1630–1670)**

1670 • London, London, , England

Age 18 — Arrival

1671-1672 • Virginia

The son, John, who went to America

Age 18 — Birth of Half-Sister <u>Martha Haddock</u>**(1672–1722)**

1672 • London, London, England

Age 18 — Birth of Half-Sister <u>Martha Haddock</u>**(1672–)**

1672 • London, London, England

Age 19 — Birth of Half-Brother <u>Richard HADDOCK Capt</u>**(1673–1751)**

1673 • All Hallows Barking, London, , England

Age 27 — Birth of Half-Brother <u>William Haddock Sr.</u>**(1681–)**

1681 • London, Middlesex, England

Age 29 — Birth of Half-Sister Elizabeth Haddock(1683–1709)

1683 • London, London, England

Age 31 — Birth of Half-Brother Joseph Haddock Captain(1684–1746)

08 May 1684 • London, London, England

Age 32 — Birth of Half-Brother Admiral Nicholas Haddock(1685–1746)

8 November 1685 • London, Middlesex, England

Age 39 — Religion

27 Jun 1692 • Middlesex County, England

Refused to take the oath of fidelity (to English crown?) and listed as a reputed papist (loyal to Pope) in parish of St. James, Westminister. Also listed as a victualler, probably supplying to the English Navy, on Sherwood St - probably a different John.

Age 39 — Residence

Jun 1692 • St James Westminster

records of address & occupation in England - probably a different John, since this one migrated early to Virginia.

Age 48 — Occupation

24 Jun 1701 • Prince George Co, Maryland, United States

Admitted to practice law in this county, where his brother, James, also practiced.

Age 55 — Death of Half-Sister Elizabeth Haddock(1683–1709)

Feb 26, 1709

Age 61 — Death of Father Sir Admiral Richard HADDOCK(1629–1715)

26 Jan 1715 • All Hallows Barking, London, Middlesex, England

Age 64 — Marriage

01 Sep 1717 • Saint Marys,,Maryland,USA

She was about 39 (about 24 yrs younger) when she married him. Her family was already established in the America's.

Elizabeth Abell

(1677–1750)

Age 67 — Birth of Son <u>JOHN II G HADDOCK</u>**(1720–1809)**

May 26 1720 • St Mary's, St Mary's County, MD, USA

Age 68 — Death of Half-Sister <u>Martha Haddock</u>**(1672–1722)**

24 Jan 1722 • St Dunstan and All Saints, Stepney County, Middlesex Borough, En

Age 71 — Birth of Son <u>William Admiral Haddock</u>**(1725–1764)**

1725 • St. Mary's County, Maryland, USA

Age 75 — Death of Sister <u>Elizabeth Haddock</u>**(1653–1728)**

1728

Age 75 — Death

1728 • Saint Mary's City, Saint Mary's County, MD, USA-Trinity Church Cem.

Age 75 — Death *(Alternate)*

1728 • Saint Mary's City, St. Mary's County, Maryland, USA

Age 75 — Burial

1728 • Saint Mary's City, St. Mary's County, Maryland, USA

Appendix III - John II G Haddock

Relation to author: 6th great grandfather

Facts

Age 0 — Birth

May 26 1720 • St Mary's, St Mary's County, MD, USA

Birth (Alternate)

1715 • St Mary's, St Mary's County, MD, USA

Age 4 — Birth of Brother William Admiral Haddock(1725–1764)

1725 • St. Mary's County, Maryland, USA

Age 8 — Death of Father John I Haddock(1653–1728)

1728 • Saint Mary's City, Saint Mary's County, MD, USA-Trinity Church Cem.

Age 21 — Birth of Son Andrew Haddock Sr.(1742–1793)

1742 • Chicod, Pitt County, NC, USA

Age 22 — Marriage

1742 • Pitt, North Carolina, USA

Liscom Hall Taylor

(1721–1802)

Age 22 — Marriage

1742 • Pitt, North Carolina, USA

(1721–1802)

Age 23 — Birth of Son JOHN III G Haddock(1744–1822)

1744 • Haddock, Pitt, North Carolina, USA

Age 24 — Birth of Son William Haddock(1745–1821)

1745 • Pitt County, NC

Age 25 — Mentioned in Will

1745 • St Mary's County, Maryland, USA

His step-father's will - Pickering

Age 25 — Birth of Daughter Elizabeth Haddock(1746–1807)

1746 • Pitt, North Carolina, United States

Age 30 — Death of Mother Elizabeth Abell(1677–1750)

1750 • Saint Mary's City, St. Mary's County, Maryland, USA

Age 30 — Birth of Son Zachariah I Haddock(1751–1825)

1751 • Chicod, Pitt County, North Carolina

Age 31 — Residence

1751 • Michaelmass, Prince William County, VA

There is a John Haddox listed in city of Michaelmass, Prince William County, VA records with dates, 1751-52 on it. Not sure if these are birth dates or what. Could be evidence of John I in that area....

Age 34 — Birth of Son CHARLES (1755) M HADDOCK(1755–1820)

1755 • Pitt County, NC, USA

Age 35 — Residence

1755 • Beaufort County, NC

Age 36 — Birth of Son Richard W Haddock(1757–1830)

1757 • Pitt County, NC, USA

Age 37 — Land Transaction

1757 • Pitt Co, North Carolina, USA

Given below is one of the earliest deeds for John Haddock- taken from the text of Haddock Heritage, Second Edition, pub 2003, by Donna Haddock Cooper. In 1757, a deed was located in North Carolina in Beaufort/Pitt Co., NC, and, in abstract

Age 42 — Residence

1762 • Early Tax List, Pitt County, NC

Age 43 — Birth of Daughter Nancy Haddock(1764–1826)

1764 • Chicod, Pitt County, NC, USA

Age 43 — Birth of Son Peter Haddock(1764–1820)

1764 • Pitt County, NC, USA

Age 44 — Residence

1764 • No Township Listed, Pitt County, NC

Age 44 — Death of Brother William Admiral Haddock(1725–1764)

1764 • Rowan County, NC, USA

Age 44 — Birth of Daughter Liscomb Taylor Haddock(1765–1845)

1765 • Chicod, Pitt County, NC, USA

Age 70 — Residence

1790 • Pitt, North Carolina, United States

at 70, 2 adults over 16 (he & wife) plus 4 white males under 16 & a total of 5 white females. This would account for him & wife, 4 sons & 4 daughters still living at home.

Age 72 — Death of Son Andrew Haddock Sr.(1742–1793)

15 May 1793 • Caswell County, NC, USA-Glens Grove Bap. Church Cem.

Age 80 — Residence

1800 • Greenville, Pitt, North Carolina

Age 82 — Death of Wife Liscom Hall Taylor(1721–1802)

26 Dec 1802 • Haddock Plantation, Pitt, North Carolina, United States

Age 87 — Death of Daughter Elizabeth Haddock(1746–1807)

1807

Age 89 — Death

29 Sep 1809 • Chicod, Pitt County, NC, USA-Haddock Plantation Fam Cem.

Cemetery notes and/or description: This is a family burial plot located on the old Haddock Plantation property at Chicod, Pitt County, North Carolina, USA. It is also known as the Mack Smith Family Cemetery, Adams Graveyard, and Adams-Smith Cemetery.

Burial

1809 • Chicod, Pitt County, North Carolina, USA

Age 30 — Birth of Son Admiral Haddock NC group(1750–1820)

1750 - OLDEST • Pitt County, NC, USA

Appendix IV - John III G Haddock

Relation to author: 5th great grandfather

Facts

Age 0 — Birth

1744 • Haddock,Pitt,North Carolina,USA

Birth *(Alternate)*

1744 • Chicod, Pitt County, NC, USA

Birth *(Alternate)*

1744 • Haddock, Pitt, North Carolina, USA

Age 1 — Birth of Brother William Haddock**(1745–1821)**

1745 • Pitt County,NC

Age 2 — Birth of Sister Elizabeth Haddock**(1746–1807)**

1746 • Pitt, North Carolina, United States

Age 7 — Birth of Brother Zachariah I Haddock**(1751–1825)**

1751 • Chicod, Pitt County, North Carolina

Age 8 — Land Transaction

10 Jul 1752 • North Carolina, United States

Sell convey and confirm unto the said Hadock [sic] his heirs and assigns a parcel of land containing one hundred acres, being part of 300 acres as by patent dated July 10th, 1752

Age 8 — Land Transaction

Jul 10, 1752 • North Carolina, United States

Sell convey and confirm unto the said Hadock [sic] his heirs and assigns a parcel of land containing one hundred acres, being part of 300 acres as by patent dated July 10th, 1752

Age 11 — Birth of Brother CHARLES (1755) M HADDOCK**(1755–1820)**

1755 • Pitt County, NC, USA

Age 13 — Birth of Brother Richard W Haddock**(1757–1830)**

1757 • Pitt County, NC, USA

Age 18 — Residence

1762 • Pitt County, NC

Age 20 — Birth of Sister <u>Nancy Haddock</u>**(1764–1826)**

1764 • Chicod, Pitt County, NC, USA

Age 20 — Birth of Brother <u>Peter Haddock</u>**(1764–1820)**

1764 • Pitt County, NC, USA

Age 21 — Birth of Sister <u>Liscomb Taylor Haddock</u>**(1765–1845)**

1765 • Chicod, Pitt County, NC, USA

Age 22 — Marriage

04 May 1766 • Pitt, North Carolina, United States

<u>Rhoda Catherine Taylor</u>

(1743–1809)

Age 23 — Birth of Son <u>John William Haddock</u>**(1767–1822)**

1767 • Chicod, Pitt County, North Carolina, USA

Age 25 — Birth of Daughter <u>Elizabeth Haddock</u>**(1769–1822)**

1769 • Chicod, Pitt County, NC, USA

Age 28 — Birth of Daughter <u>Nancy Haddock</u>**(1772–1820)**

1772 • , Pitt, North Carolina, USA

Age 30 — Birth of Son <u>Admiral Haddock Georgia Group</u>**(1774–1860)**

1774 • Chicod, Pitt County, North Carolina, USA

Age 34 — Birth of Son <u>William Haddock</u>**(1778–1845)**

1778 • North Carolina, United States

Age 35 — Birth of Son <u>Zachariah II Haddock</u>**(1779–1842)**

10 Jun 1779 • Pitt County, North Carolina, USA

Age 36 — Birth of Son <u>Charles (1780) Haddock</u>**(1780–1859)**

1780 • Chicod, Pitt, North Carolina, United States

Age 36 — Birth of Daughter Esther Haddock**(1780–1870)**

12 May 1780 • Pitt County, North Carolina, USA

Age 42 — Birth of Half-Brother Naseby Hall HADDOCK**(1786–1859)**

1786

Age 46 — Birth of Daughter Elizabeth Haddock**(1790–1872)**

1790

Age 46 — Birth of Son Henry Haddock**(1790–1799)**

1790 • Chicod, Pitt County, North Carolina, USA

Age 46 — Residence

1790 • Pitt, North Carolina, United States

Admiral, William, Charles, & John all shown on same page in 1790 Pitt Co. Census. Also, Mills & Buck families lived near.

Age 49 — Death of Brother Andrew Haddock Sr.**(1742–1793)**

15 May 1793 • Caswell County, NC, USA-Glens Grove Bap. Church Cem.

Age 55 — Death of Son Henry Haddock**(1790–1799)**

1799 • Chicod, Pitt County, North Carolina, USA

Age 56 — Residence

1800 • Greenville, Pitt, North Carolina

at 56, Census shows John senior & son of John senior living next to each other with a son & 2 daughters still living w/them. 10 yrs later, Issac Buck & Fredrick Mills still lived next to them.

Age 58 — Death of Mother Liscom Hall Taylor**(1721–1802)**

26 Dec 1802 • Haddock Plantation, Pitt, North Carolina, United States

Age 63 — Death of Sister Elizabeth Haddock**(1746–1807)**

1807

Age 65 — Death of Father JOHN II G HADDOCK**(1720–1809)**

29 Sep 1809 • Chicod, Pitt County, NC, USA-Haddock Plantation Fam Cem.

Age 65 — Death *(Alternate)*

Sep 29, 1809 • Haddock, Jones, Georgia, USA

Age 65 — Land

1809 • Jones County, GA

There, an Admiral "Hadduck" filed claim on Cherokee land in Jones County, Georgia and a John Haddock filed 2 claims in Pulaski County. I think this is John III. (source: http://www.usgwarchives.net/ga/gafiles.htm)

Age 65 — Death of Wife <u>Rhoda Catherine Taylor</u>**(1743–1809)**

1809 • Haddock, Jones, Georgia, USA

Age 66 — Residence

1810 • Pitt, North Carolina, United States

Abt 1809, moved with his son, Admiral, to South Carolina after the death of his father.

Age 76 — Death of Brother <u>Peter Haddock</u>**(1764–1820)**

Sep 04, 1820 • Double Branch, Fulton County, GA, USA-Haddock Family Cem Jones County

Age 76 — Death of Brother <u>CHARLES (1755) M HADDOCK</u>**(1755–1820)**

Sep 12, 1820 • Pulaski County, GA, USA

Age 76 — Residence

1820 • Columbus, North Carolina, United States

Age 76 — Death of Daughter <u>Nancy Haddock</u>**(1772–1820)**

1820 • Knox, Kentucky, United States

Age 76 — Death of Brother <u>Admiral Haddock NC group</u>**(1750–1820)**

1820 • Collecton County, SC, USA-Mack Smith Fam Cem

Age 77 — Death of Brother <u>William Haddock</u>**(1745–1821)**

11 Sep 1821 • Pitt, North Carolina, United States

Age 77 — Death *(Alternate)*

1821 • Haddock, Jones, Georgia, United States

Age 78 — Death of Son <u>John William Haddock</u>**(1767–1822)**

1822 • Chicod, Pitt County, NC, USA-Haddock Plantation Fam Cem.

Age 78 — Death of Daughter <u>Elizabeth Haddock</u>**(1769–1822)**

1822 • Edgecombe, Edgecombe County, NC, USA- Haddock Plantation Fam Cem.

Age 78 — Death

1822 • Haddock, Jones County, GA,USA-Haddock Family Cem.

Age 78 — Death *(Alternate)*

1822 • Haddock, Jones, Georgia, USA

Age 78 — Death *(Alternate)*

1822 • Haddock, Jones, Georgia, United States

Age 78 — Burial

1822 • Haddock, Jones County, Georgia, USA

Age 6 — Birth of Brother <u>Admiral Haddock NC group</u>**(1750–1820)**

1750 - OLDEST • Pitt County, NC, USA

Appendix V - *John William Haddock*

Relation to author: 4th great grandfather

Facts

Age 0 — Birth

1767 • Chicod, Pitt County, North Carolina, USA

Age 2 — Birth of Sister <u>Elizabeth Haddock</u>**(1769–1822)**

1769 • Chicod, Pitt County, NC, USA

Age 4 — Birth of Sister <u>Nancy Haddock</u>**(1772–1820)**

1772 • , Pitt, North Carolina, USA

Age 7 — Birth of Brother <u>Admiral Haddock Georgia Group</u>**(1774–1860)**

1774 • Chicod, Pitt County, North Carolina, USA

Age 11 — Birth of Brother <u>William Haddock</u>**(1778–1845)**

1778 • North Carolina, United States

Age 12 — Birth of Brother <u>Zachariah II Haddock</u>**(1779–1842)**

10 Jun 1779 • Pitt County, North Carolina, USA

Age 12 — Birth of Brother <u>Charles (1780) Haddock</u>**(1780–1859)**

1780 • Chicod, Pitt, North Carolina, United States

Age 13 — Birth of Sister <u>Esther Haddock</u>**(1780–1870)**

12 May 1780 • Pitt County, North Carolina, USA

Age 19 — Birth of Son <u>Nasby Hall Haddock</u>**(1786–1859)**

1786 • Swift Creek, Pitt, North Carolina, United States

Age 19 — Marriage

1786 • , Pitt, North Carolina, USA

It looks like his wife, Nancy's cousin, Sarah, married his son, Nasby Hall Haddock in 1803. Possible confusion.

Both are our direct descendants. No source citation>

<u>Nancy Mills</u>

(1768–1830)

Age 20 — Birth of Daughter Liscom Haddock**(1788–1845)**

1788 • Swift Creek, Pitt, North Carolina, United States

Age 23 — Birth of Sister Elizabeth Haddock**(1790–1872)**

1790

Age 23 — Birth of Brother Henry Haddock**(1790–1799)**

1790 • Chicod, Pitt County, North Carolina, USA

Age 32 — Death of Brother Henry Haddock**(1790–1799)**

1799 • Chicod, Pitt County, North Carolina, USA

Age 33 — Residence

1800 • Greenville, Pitt, North Carolina

Age 42 — Death of Mother Rhoda Catherine Taylor**(1743–1809)**

1809 • Haddock, Jones, Georgia, USA

Age 43 — Residence

1810 • Pitt, North Carolina, United States

abt 45, shows still living in Pitt Co with a total of 7 people in house.

Age 53 — Death of Sister Nancy Haddock**(1772–1820)**

1820 • Knox, Kentucky, United States

Age 55 — Death of Father JOHN III G Haddock**(1744–1822)**

1822 • Haddock, Jones County, GA,USA-Haddock Family Cem.

Age 55 — Death of Sister Elizabeth Haddock**(1769–1822)**

1822 • Edgecombe, Edgecombe County, NC, USA- Haddock Plantation Fam Cem.

Age 55 — Death

1822 • Chicod, Pitt County, NC, USA-Haddock Plantation Fam Cem.

Buried in Mack Smith Cemetery, family cemetery.

Appendix VI - Nasby Hall Haddock

Relation to author: 3rd great grandfather

Facts

Age 0 — Birth

1786 • Swift Creek, Pitt, North Carolina, United States

Age 1 — Birth of Sister Liscom Haddock**(1788–1845)**

1788 • Swift Creek, Pitt, North Carolina, United States

Age 18 — Marriage

1804 • Pitt, North Carolina, United States

Looks like he married his mother's sister. Only one marriage, apparently. No source citation>

Sarah (Sary) B Mills

(1788–1866)

Age 18 — Birth of Son JORDAN DAVID HADDOCK Sr.**(1805–1861)**

1805 • Chicod, Pitt County, NC, USA

Age 21 — Birth of Daughter Alice Haddock**(1808–)**

1808 • Pitt, North Carolina, United States

Age 23 — Birth of Son Naseby Haddock**(1810–)**

1810

Age 31 — Birth of Son Nathen Spencer Haddock**(1818–1867)**

1818 • Swift Creek, Pitt, North Carolina, United States

Age 34 — Residence

1820 • Capt Brooks District, Pitt, North Carolina, United States

Age 36 — Death of Father John William Haddock**(1767–1822)**

1822 • Chicod, Pitt County, NC, USA-Haddock Plantation Fam Cem.

Age 36 — Birth of Son Burton Hall Haddock Sr**(1823–1880)**

1823 • Pitt, North Carolina, United States

Age 36 — Birth of Son <u>William HAUL "Nasby" Haddock Sr.</u>**(1823–1913)**

Jan 1823 • North Carolina, United States

Age 37 — Birth of Son <u>William Haul Haddock</u>**(1824–1868)**

1824 • North Carolina, United States

Age 38 — Birth of Daughter <u>Haddock F</u>**(1825–)**

1825

Age 38 — Birth of Daughter <u>Haddock F</u>**(1825–)**

1825

Age 39 — Birth of Son <u>Joseph A Haddock</u>**(1826–1875)**

1826 • Pitt, North Carolina, United States

Age 44 — Residence

1830 • Pitt, North Carolina, USA

Age 44 — Death of Mother <u>Nancy Mills</u>**(1768–1830)**

1830 • Chicod, Pitt County, NC, USA-Haddock Plantation Family Cem.

Age 45 — Birth of Daughter <u>Ritty Haddock</u>**(1832–1880)**

1832 • Pitt County, NC

Age 54 — Residence

1840 • Pitt, North Carolina, United States

Age 59 — Death of Sister <u>Liscom Haddock</u>**(1788–1845)**

Dec 26, 1845 • Wayne, Georgia, United States

Age 59 — Death of Half-Sister <u>Liscomb Taylor Haddock</u>**(1765–1845)**

Dec 26, 1845 • Wayne County, GA, USA

Age 73 — Death

Jun 1859 • Trenton, Jones, North Carolina, USA

Haddock Family Cemetery

Burial

1859 • Trenton, Jones County, North Carolina, USA

Haddock Family Cemetery

Appendix VII - Jordan David Haddock, Sr.

Relation to author: 2nd great grandfather

Facts

Age 0 — Birth

1805 • Chicod, Pitt County, NC, USA

Birth *(Alternate)*

Abt. 1805 • Pitt County, North Carolina, USA

Age 24 — Marriage

1829 • Pitt, North Carolina, United States

They lived around the Buck family & there were at least two generations of Bucks who married Haddocks.

SARAH CLEMENTINE "CLEMMIE" BUCK

(1812–1893)

Age 25 — Residence

1830 • Pitt, North Carolina, USA

Age 35 — Residence

1840 • Pitt, North Carolina, United States

Age 45 — Residence

1850 • Cache, St Francis, Arkansas, USA

Age 55 — Residence

1860 • Gainsburro Township, Independence County, AR

Age 56 — Death

18 Mar 1861 • Batesville, Independence County, AR, USA-Liberty Cem.

Burial

1861 • Sulphur Rock, Independence County, Arkansas, USA

after death

after death

Appendix VIII - Calvin Cash Haddock

Relation to author: Great grandfather

Facts

Age 0 — Birth

07 Dec 1845 • Chicod, Pitt County, North Carolina, USA

Birth *(Alternate)*

7 Dec 1845 • Chicod, Pitt County, NC, USA

Age 2 — Birth of Sister Clessonie Haddock**(1848–1924)**

1848 • Pitt, North Carolina, United States

Age 2 — Birth of Sister Elizabeth Clementine "Clemmy" Haddock**(1848–1917)**

14 Apr 1848 • Pitt County, NC, USA

Age 5 — Residence

1850 • Cache, St Francis, Arkansas

Age 5 — Birth of Brother William Pleas Haddock**(1851–1930)**

17 Apr 1851 • Independence, Arkansas, United States

Age 6 — Birth of Sister Lucinda "Lou" Haddock**(1852–1894)**

1852 • St Francis, Arkansas, United States

Age 7 — Birth of Brother Hiram Haddock**(1853–1860)**

1853 • Arkansas City, Arkansas County, AR, USA

Age 15 — Residence

1860 • Gainsboro, Independence, Arkansas, United States

Age in 1860: 16

Age 15 — Death of Brother Hiram Haddock**(1853–1860)**

1860 • Arkansas City, Arkansas County, AR, USA-Haddock Cem.

Age 15 — Death of Father <u>JORDAN DAVID HADDOCK Sr.</u>**(1805–1861)**

18 Mar 1861 • Batesville, Independence County, AR, USA-Liberty Cem.

Age 16 — Residence

1861-1865 • USA

Civil War service

Age 17 — Death of Brother <u>Ransom "Ranse" Haddock</u>**(1834–1863)**

Mar 10, 1863 • Iron, Iron, Missouri, United States

Age 19 — Death of Sister <u>Harriett Ann Haddock</u>**(1832–1865)**

Mar 18, 1865 • Batesville, Independence County, AR, USA-Haddock Cem.

Age 21 — Marriage

30 Dec 1866 • Independence, Arkansas, United States

1866

<u>Virginia Elizabeth Nesbit</u>

(1849–1937)

Age 22 — Birth of Daughter <u>Margaret A. V. Haddock</u>**(1868–1868)**

10 Jan 1868 • Independence, Arkansas, United States

Age 22 — Death of Daughter <u>Margaret A. V. Haddock</u>**(1868–1868)**

15 Jan 1868 • Batesville, Independence County, Arkansas, USA

Age 23 — Birth of Daughter <u>Cordelia Carolina Haddock</u>**(1869–1872)**

Apr 25, 1869 • Batesville, Independence, Arkansas, United States

Age 25 — Residence

1870 • Gainsboro, Independence, Arkansas, United States

Age in 1870: 24

Age 25 — Residence

1870 • Gainsboro, Independence, Arkansas, United States

Age in 1870: 24

Age 25 — Residence

1870 • Gainsboro, Independence, Arkansas, United States

Age in 1870: 24

Age 25 — Residence

1870 • Gainsboro, Independence, Arkansas, United States

Age in 1870: 24

Age 25 — Residence

1870 • Gainsboro, Independence, Arkansas, United States

Age in 1870: 24

Age 25 — Residence

1870 • Gainsboro, Independence, Arkansas, United States

Age in 1870: 24

Age 25 — Residence

1870 • Batesville, Independence, Arkansas

1870 Census

Age 25 — Birth of Daughter <u>Virginia Elizabeth "Jennie" Haddock</u>**(1871–1898)**

1871 • Batesville, Independence County, AR, USA

Age 26 — Death of Daughter <u>Cordelia Carolina Haddock</u>**(1869–1872)**

Oct 25, 1872 • Batesville, Independence County, AR, USA-Liberty Cem.

Age 27 — Birth of Daughter <u>Lilly M. Haddock</u>**(1873–1890)**

1873 • Batesville, Independence County, AR, USA

Age 29 — Birth of Daughter <u>Louisa Lizziebeth Elizabeth Haddock</u>**(1875–1973)**

11 Nov 1875 • Batesville, Independence, Arkansas, United States

Age 34 — Death of Brother <u>Jordan David Haddock Jr.</u>**(1840–1880)**

Jun 01, 1880 • Independence, Arkansas, United States

1880 • Gainsboro, Independence, Arkansas, United States

Age 35 — Birth of Son Nesbitt Haddock**(1881—1884)**

Dec 1881 • Independence, Arkansas, United States

Age 37 — Birth of Daughter Tommie Ann Haddock**(1882–1986)**

12 Dec 1882 • Batesville, Independence County, AR, USA

Age 38 — Birth of Daughter Ruth Loucinda Haddock**(1884–1967)**

20 Jun 1884 • Independence, Arkansas, United States

Age 38 — Death of Son Nesbitt Haddock**(1881–1884)**

Aug 25, 1884 • Batesville, Independence County, AR, USA-Liberty Cem.

Age 41 — Birth of Son William David (Dave) Haddock**(1887–1948)**

22 Nov 1887 • Batesville, Independence County, AR, USA

Age 44 — Birth of Daughter Martha A F Haddock**(1890–1890)**

1890 • Independence, Arkansas, United States

Age 44 — Death of Daughter Martha A F Haddock**(1890–1890)**

Aug 25, 1890 • Batesville, Independence County, AR, USA-Liberty Cem.

Age 44 — Death of Daughter Lilly M. Haddock**(1873–1890)**

19 Oct 1890 • Batesville, Independence County, AR, USA-Bethel Cem

Age 47 — Death of Mother SARAH CLEMENTINE "CLEMMIE" BUCK**(1812–1893)**

23 Mar 1893 • Independence, Arkansas, United States

Age 48 — Birth of Daughter Kathryn Kate Haddock**(1894–1989)**

02 Sep 1894 • Hot Springs, Garland County, AR, USA

Age 49 — Death of Sister Lucinda "Lou" Haddock**(1852–1894)**

1894 • Batesville, Independence County, Arkansas, USA

Age 52 — Death of Daughter Virginia Elizabeth "Jennie" Haddock**(1871–1898)**

Jun 1898 • Batesville, Independence County, AR, USA-Bethel Cem.

Age 54 — Death of Brother <u>Noah Uriah Haddock</u>**(1842–1900)**

Mar 08, 1900 • Batesville, Independence, Arkansas, United States

Age 55 — Residence

1900 • Gainsboro, Independence, Arkansas, USA

Marital Status: Married; Relation to Head of House: Head

Age 65 — Residence

1910 • Justice Precinct 4, Hopkins, Texas

Age 65 — Death of Sister <u>Louisa Elizabeth Haddock Buck</u>**(1833–1910)**

1910 • Cooper, Delta, Texas, United States

Age 75 — Residence

1920 • Commerce, Hunt, Texas

Age 78 — Death of Sister <u>Clessonie Haddock</u>**(1848–1924)**

Mar 13, 1924 • Beaver Dam, Pitt, North Carolina

Age 81 — Death

28 Feb 1927 • Commerce, Hunt County, TX, USA-Rosemound Cem.

Age 81 — Death *(Alternate)*

28 Feb 1927 • Commerce, Hunt, Texas, USA

Mar 17, 1927 • Hunt

Burial

1927 • Commerce, Hunt County, Texas, USA

Rosemound Cemetery

Appendix IX - William David (Dave) Haddock

Relation to author: grandfather

Facts

Age 0 — Birth

22 Nov 1887 • Batesville, Independence County, AR, USA

Memorial stone located at Mt Zion Cemetery in Hopkins County by his first wife.

Age 2 — Birth of Sister Martha A F Haddock**(1890–1890)**

1890 • Independence, Arkansas, United States

Age 2 — Death of Sister Martha A F Haddock**(1890–1890)**

Aug 25, 1890 • Batesville, Independence County, AR, USA-Liberty Cem.

Age 2 — Death of Sister Lilly M. Haddock**(1873–1890)**

19 Oct 1890 • Batesville, Independence County, AR, USA-Bethel Cem

Age 6 — Birth of Sister Kathryn Kate Haddock**(1894–1989)**

02 Sep 1894 • Hot Springs, Garland County, AR, USA

Age 10 — Death of Sister Virginia Elizabeth "Jennie" Haddock**(1871–1898)**

Jun 1898 • Batesville, Independence County, AR, USA-Bethel Cem.

Age 13 — Residence

1900 • Gainsboro Township, Independence, Arkansas

Age 20 — 1st Marriage

22 Nov 1908 • Hopkins, Texas, United States

Flora Gertrude "Trudy" Raines

(1891–1921)

Age 21 — Birth of Daughter Zoia Avaline Haddock**(1909–2008)**

1 Aug 1909 • Hopkins Co., Tx

Age 22 — Birth of Son William Marvin Haddock**(1910–1965)**

28 Aug 1910 • Hopkins County, Texas, USA

Age 23 — Residence

1910 • Justice Precinct 4, Hopkins, Texas

Age 29 — Birth of Daughter Mattie Virginia Haddock**(1917–2013)**

06 Oct 1917 • Branom, Hopkins County, TX, USA

Age 30 — Residence

1917-1918 • Hopkins, Texas

Age 31 — Birth of Daughter Minnie Elizabeth Haddock**(1919–2008)**

19 Feb 1919 • Sulphur Springs, Hopkins County, TX, USA

Age 32 — Birth of Daughter Mamie Ruth Haddock**(1920–1920)**

8 May 1920 • Hopkins, Texas, United States

Age 32 — Death of Daughter Mamie Ruth Haddock**(1920–1920)**

29 May 1920 • Branom, Hopkins County, TX, USA-Mt. Zion Cem.

Age 33 — Residence

1920 • Justice Precinct 4, Hopkins, Texas

Marital Status: Married; Relation to Head of House: Head

Age 33 — Death of Wife Flora Gertrude "Trudy" Raines**(1891–1921)**

18 Nov 1921 • Branom, Hopkins County, TX, USA-Mt. Zion Cem.

Age 35 — **2nd** Marriage

17 Jun 1923 • Commerce, Hunt, Texas, United States

Nunnie Mae McManus

(1904–1967)

Age 35 — Marriage

17 Jun 1923 • Commerce, Hunt, Texas, United States

Age 36 — Birth of Daughter Margaret Bernice Haddock**(1924–2015)**

1 August 1924 • Texas

Age 38 — Birth of Daughter Helen Louise Haddock**(1926–1994)**

15 Aug 1926 • Jacobe, Hunt County, Texas

Age 39 — Death of Father <u>Calvin Cash Haddock</u>**(1845–1927)**

28 Feb 1927 • Commerce, Hunt County, TX, USA-Rosemound Cem.

Age 41 — Birth of Daughter <u>Nelda Myril Haddock</u>**(1929–)**

24 Aug 1929 • Hunt County, TX, USA

Age 43 — Residence

1930 • Precinct 1, Hunt, Texas

Age: 42; Marital Status: Married; Relation to Head of House: Head

Age 43 — Birth of Son <u>William David "W D" Haddock Jr</u>**(1931–)**

04 Mar 1931 • Ridgeway, Hopkins County, TX, USA

Age 47 — Birth of Daughter <u>Zoie "Oleta" Haddock</u>**(1934–2016)**

17 Dec 1934 • Ridgeway, Hopkins County, TX, USA

Age 48 — Residence

1935 • Rural, Hopkins, Texas

Age 49 — Birth of Daughter <u>Mary Oretha Haddock</u>**(1937–)**

1937 • Ridgeway, Hopkins County, TX, USA

Age 49 — Death of Mother <u>Virginia Elizabeth Nesbit</u>**(1849–1937)**

24 Jan 1937 • Ridgeway, Hopkins County, Texas, USA

Age 52 — Birth of Daughter <u>Shirley Jo Haddock</u>**(1940–1990)**

16 Feb 1940 • Klondike, TX

Age 52 — Residence

01 Apr 1940 • Delta, Texas, USA

Marital Status: Married; Relation to Head of House: Head

Age 52 — Residence

01 Apr 1940 • Delta, Texas, USA

Marital Status: Married; Relation to Head of House: Head

Age 52 — Residence

Apr 01, 1940 • Delta, Texas, USA

Marital Status: Married Relation to Head of House: Head

Age 53 — Race

Mar 1941

White - Social Security

Age 55 — Residence

1942 • Klondike, Texas, USA

Age 56 — Birth of Daughter Patricia Mae Haddock**(1944–2009)**

16 Oct 1944 • Petty, Lamar County, TX, USA

Age 61 — Death

10 Dec 1948 • Commerce, Texas

Age:61 FAG #5054985

Residence

1948 • Commerce, Hunt, Texas

at time of death

Burial

1948 • Commerce, Hunt County, TX, USA-Rosemond Cem.

Appendix X - William Marvin Haddock

Relation to author: Father

Facts:

Age 0 — Birth

28 Aug 1910 • Hopkins County, Texas, USA

Age 7 — Birth of Sister <u>Mattie Virginia Haddock</u>**(1917–2013)**

06 Oct 1917 • Branom, Hopkins County, TX, USA

Age 8 — Birth of Sister <u>Minnie Elizabeth Haddock</u>**(1919–2008)**

19 Feb 1919 • Sulphur Springs, Hopkins County, TX, USA

Age 9 — Birth of Sister <u>Mamie Ruth Haddock</u>**(1920–1920)**

8 May 1920 • Hopkins, Texas, United States

Age 9 — Death of Sister <u>Mamie Ruth Haddock</u>**(1920–1920)**

29 May 1920 • Branom, Hopkins County, TX, USA-Mt. Zion Cem.

Age 10 — Residence

1920 • Justice Precinct 4, Hopkins, Texas

Marital Status: Single Relation to Head of House: Son

Age 11 — Death of Mother <u>Flora Gertrude "Trudy" Raines</u>**(1891–1921)**

18 Nov 1921 • Branom, Hopkins County, TX, USA-Mt. Zion Cem.

Age 13 — Birth of Half-Sister <u>Margaret Bernice Haddock</u>**(1924–2015)**

1 August 1924 • Texas

Age 15 — Birth of Half-Sister <u>Helen Louise Haddock</u>**(1926–1994)**

15 Aug 1926 • Jacobe, Hunt County, Texas

Age 18 — Birth of Half-Sister <u>Nelda Myril Haddock</u>**(1929–)**

24 Aug 1929 • Hunt County, TX, USA

Age 18 — Birth of Half-Sister <u>Nelda Myril Haddock</u>**(1929–)**

24 Aug 1929 • Jacobe, Hunt County, TX, USA

Age 20 — Residence

1930 • Precinct 1, Hunt, Texas, USA

Marital Status: Single Relation to Head of House: Son

Age 20 — Residence

1930 • Precinct 1, Hunt, Texas, USA

Marital Status: Single; Relation to Head of House: Son

Age 20 — Residence

1930 • Precinct 1, Hunt, Texas

Age 20 — Residence

1930 • Precinct 1, Hunt, Texas

Age 20 — Residence

1930 • Precinct 1, Hunt, Texas

Age 20 — Residence

1930 • Precinct 1, Hunt, Texas

Age 20 — Residence

1930 • Precinct 1, Hunt, Texas

Age 20 — Birth of Half-Brother <u>W D Haddock</u>**(1931–)**

04 Mar 1931 • Ridgeway, Hopkins County, TX, USA

Age 20 — Birth of Half-Brother <u>William David "W D" Haddock Jr</u>**(1931–)**

04 Mar 1931 • Ridgeway, Hopkins County, TX, USA

Age 22 — Marriage

05 Nov 1932 • Hopkins co., Texas

<u>ELSIE MARIE PIPKIN</u>

(1916–1953)

Age 22 — Marriage

05 Nov 1932 • Branom, Hopkins, Texas, United States

1st marriage

ELSIE MARIE PIPKIN

(1916–1953)

Age 24 — Birth of Half-Sister Zoie "Oleta" Haddock**(1934–2016)**

17 Dec 1934 • Ridgeway, Hopkins County, TX, USA

Age 25 — Birth of Daughter Odessa Faye Haddock Jackman**(1935–)**

Oct 31, 1935 • Hunt County, TX, USA

Age 25 — Residence

1935 • Rural, Hunt, Texas

Age 26 — Birth of Half-Sister Mary Oretha Haddock**(1937–)**

1937 • Ridgeway, Hopkins County, TX, USA

Age 28 — Birth of Daughter Maredia Maye Haddock Cunningham**(1939–)**

Jan 27, 1939 • Cooper Hospital, Delta County, TX, USA

Age 29 — Birth of Half-Sister Shirley Jo Haddock**(1940–1990)**

16 Feb 1940 • Klondike, TX

01 Apr 1940 • Delta, Texas, United States

Age: 29; Marital Status: Married; Relation to Head of House: Head

Age 29 — Residence

Age 30 — Birth and Death of Son William Walter Haddock**(1940–1940)**

28 Nov 1940 • Miller Grove, Hopkins County, TX, USA

Age 32 — Birth of Son Marvin Clifton Haddock**(1943–**

22 Jan 1943 • Hopkins County, Texas, USA

Age 33 — Birth of Son Nolan Oneal Haddock**(1944–2004)**

24 Jul 1944 • Petty, Lamar County, TX, USA

Age 34 — Birth of Half-Sister Patricia Mae Haddock**(1944–2009)**

16 Oct 1944 • Petty, Lamar County, TX, USA

Age 37 — Birth of Son <u>Billy Dan Haddock</u>**(1948–)**

13 Aug 1948 • Hopkins, Texas

Age 38 — Death of Father <u>William David (Dave) Haddock</u>**(1887–1948)**

10 Dec 1948 • Commerce, Texas

Age 39 — Birth of Son <u>William Alton Haddock</u>**(1950–)**

17 Apr 1950 • Commerce, Texas

Age 42 — Death of Wife <u>ELSIE MARIE PIPKIN</u>**(1916–1953)**

29 May 1953 • Commerce, Hunt County, TX, USA-Mt. Zion Cem Hopkins County

Age 42 — Birth of Son <u>Gary David Haddock Gunter</u>**(1953–)**

29 May 1953 • Commerce, Texas

Age 46 — Marriage

1956

2nd marriage

<u>Iler Lavay 'Vay' Gillean</u>

(1914–2012)

Age 51 — Marriage

Jun 1962 • Commerce Hunt County, TX, USA

3rd marriage

<u>Hazel Gatha Quinn</u>

(1911–2003)

Age 55 — Death

05 Sep 1965 • Commerce, Hunt County, TX, USA Hopkins County-Mt. Zion Cem.

Age:55 FAG #54752495

Residence

1965 • Commerce, Hunt, Texas

Living here at time of death

Burial

1965 • Mount Zion, Hopkins County, TX, USA-Mt Zion Cem.

Blank Charts from 1ˢᵗ Edition

FIRST EDITION

FAMILY RECORD OF THE   *FAMILY*

Full name of husband:

    Nickname: **Education:**
    Birth date: **Occupation:**
    Birth place: **Religion:**
    Death date: **Notes:**
    Burial place: **Military:**

His father: **His mother:**

    Marriage date: **Place:**

Full name of wife (maiden):

    Nickname: **Education:**
    Birth date: **Occupation:**
    Birth place: **Religion:**
    Death date: **Notes:**
    Burial place:

Her father: **Her mother:**

    Other spouses:

                                    DATE:

CHILDREN NAMES	SEX	BIRTH	DEATH	MARRIAGES (NAME & DATE)

SOURCES:

FAMILY RECORD OF THE   *FAMILY*

Full name of husband:

    Nickname: Education:
    Birth date: Occupation:
    Birth place: Religion:
    Death date: Notes:
    Burial place: Military:

His father: **His mother:**

    Marriage date: **Place:**

Full name of wife (maiden):

    Nickname: Education:
    Birth date: Occupation:
    Birth place: Religion:
    Death date: Notes:
    Burial place:

Her father: **Her mother:**

    Other spouses:

                                           DATE:

CHILDREN NAMES	SEX	BIRTH	DEATH	MARRIAGES (NAME & DATE)

SOURCES:

Appendices From First Edition

FOCUS ON THE YATES FAMILY

As we backtrack up the family line from Dave Haddock's wife, Gertrude, we see Mattie Yates, Gertrude's mother and wife of John Raines. The Yates family settled in Texas before the battle for independence from Mexico. Mattie's grandfather, Thomas Avis Yates, was originally from Missouri but moved near Paris in the general area of the Roxton community around 1835. Records reflect that he enlisted on November 13, 1835 and fought with the Volunteer Texas Army that took the Alamo from the Mexicans in the fall of 1835. This battle was known as the Bexar Campaign.

Bexar Campaign

Stephen F. Austin was originally commander-in-chief of the volunteer army, but he was chosen to represent Texas' interest in the United States, so Edward Burleson of Mina (now Bastrop) was chosen commander on November 25, 1836. Burleson had considerable military experience in Tennessee and Missouri before coming to Texas.

Many of the Texas volunteers were farmers and returned to their homes in late November, becoming discouraged. New arrivals kept the army from shrinking in size.

In early December, Burleson and his officers agreed to end the siege of San Antonio and allow the men to return to their homes. However, information from a captured Mexican officer and a Texan from San Antonio, Samuel A. Maverick,

Yates Family (from 1ˢᵗ Edition)

changed their minds. The word was that General Cos and the Mexican army were weak and could not repulse a major attack.

Ben Milam, an old impresario agent, agreed to lead the attack on San Antonio. About 300 men volunteered to follow him. Milam divided his force into two columns. He commanded one and Frank W. Johnson commanded the other.

The assault began on December 5th. The fighting lasted four days as Milam's men fought their way from house to house. On the 3rd day of the battle, Milam was killed and Johnson took command.

On December 9th, General Cos surrendered after taking refuge in the Alamo. He signed the agreement on December 10th. The Mexican forces numbered about 1300 men and were defeated by about 300 Texans. The Texans had lost only two killed and 26 wounded while 150 Mexican soldiers were killed.

In March, 1836, General Santa Anna came back to San Antonio and took the city back by defeating the Texans under William Travis in the Battle of the Alamo (Anderson & Wooster, 1972).

Records supporting Thomas Yates' service follow the narrative in this section. As they reflect, he was discharged on January 1, 1836 and was reimbursed $31.33 for his expenses on April 15, 1837 and later given two leagues of land when Texas became a Republic, one league for his army service and another for settling in Texas before 1836. I checked the land records in Hopkins County where the land was

The Haddock Family _____

located and found that Thomas Yates sold the land, over 8,000 acres, for $2,000 to a lawyer in Houston on the same day the Republic of Texas deeded it to him. The next day the lawyer sold it for a handsome profit to someone in New Orleans. This apparently was a common practice because the lawyer's name appeared several times on the deed records that year, indicating many other similar transactions.

Down the genealogical line we find **Thomas Keeling Yates** who fought in Burford's Regiment, 19th Texas Calvary and died in the Civil War. Records of his service are found on the following pages, also. Apparently, his wife, Elizabeth, died soon after his death leaving Mattie and her brothers orphans. They were reportedly taken in by Keeling's sister, Martha Ann Elizabeth, and her husband, Eli Jennings Shelton, who raised them.

Eli Jennings Shelton

Captain E.J. Shelton was a son of Jesse Shelton, a native of Kentucky. His father, Jesse, lived the first two years in a fortification near the present site of Roxton, called "Shelton's Fort", the farm of the settlers being worked by companies to protect them from Indians. A historical marker stands at the site to commemorate this time and place.

April 11, 1823, Eli was born in what is now the Choctaw Nation, Indian Territory. It was then the Territory of

The Haddock Family _____

Arkansas. He was fourteen years old when his father settled in Texas, and served the Republic of Texas in 1838 as a ranger on the frontier. May 16, 1846, he married Martha Ann Elizabeth, daughter of Thomas Avis Yates, early settlers of Texas, but originally from Missouri. Mrs. Shelton was born in Hempstead county, Arkansas, and became the mother of the following children - Alice Irene, now wife of Dr. S. N. Compton; Jesse R; Thomas B.A.; Lola Aveline, wife of S.N. Harroway; Avis Idella, widow of C.W. Shipe; and Maggie M.J., wife of David A. Coleman.

Mr. Shelton enlisted in the Confederate service, company A, Ninth Texas Infantry, in 1861, and his company was in the engagements at Corinth and Shiloh. He was then placed in Burnett's battalion of sharpshooters, and when General Maxey, who commanded the Ninth Texas, was transferred to the trans-Mississippi department, the battalion returned with Eli, who was placed in charge of the quartermaster's department at Bonham, Fannin county, where he served until the surrender. He was in the Texas legislature in 1857-58-59-60-72-73, and was a member of the session that called the convention which passed the ordinance of secession and assisted in the legislature and at home to put the State government in operation after the ordinance of secession was ratified. He was never been a public man through choice, but accepted these positions at the solicitation of friends. He was regarded by his neighbors and acquaintances as one of the

The Haddock Family _____

best citizens of the State, and took a lively interest in the Old Veteran Association, of which he was a member. Mr. Shelton was for many years a Mason and a member of the Methodist Episcopal church (Biographical Souvenir, 1889).

The above information suggests Eli and his wife were prominent citizens of Texas during this time. However, they were reported as rather cruel caretakers of Mattie and her brothers. Perhaps this is why we found Mattie's youngest brother, Rueben living with John and her in Delta County on the 1880 Census.

In any case, the Yates and Raines families seemed to be prominent citizens in the Delta and Hopkins County area. It was from this tradition that Flora Gertrude Raines came when she married William David Haddock.

SOURCES:

Anderson, A.N. & Wooster, R.A. (1972). Texas and Texans. Austin: Steck - Vaughn Co.

Biographical Souvenir. (1889). Chicago: F.A. Battey & Co.

HOPKINS COUNTY, TEXAS LAND RECORDS, Book P, page 18.

Raines Family (from 1st Edition)

FOCUS ON THE RAINES FAMILY

Little is known about the Raines family except that they were reportedly of Irish descent and moved to Texas from Kentucky. John Raines was reportedly bald. He had a brother named Will (possibly William). His sister reportedly married a man named Baker and they had a furniture business in Paris, Texas. John Allan Raines donated a piece of land on which the Mt. Zion church is located. The history of this church reveals more about the Raines family.

HISTORY OF MT. ZION CHURCHES AND CEMETERY
BRANOM COMMUNITY
HOPKINS COUNTY, TEXAS

<u>Mt. Zion Methodist Episcopal Church</u>

This information is of necessity more than the history of the two churches at Mt. Zion. In order to understand and appreciate the history of any organization, we must understand the context, the geographic area, the cause and the method of organization.

The cause could be placed on need for the organization. The method was set forth for organizing Methodist Episcopal churches, at Baltimore Maryland, December 24, 1774, by Francis Asbury and Thomas Coke who were ordained representatives of John Wesley. They divided the inhabited part of America into sections -or circuits. The Circuit Riders - or Preachers on horseback -went over areas where no

The Haddock Family _____

roads or trails marked their way to carry the gospel to the settlers.

Walter Brownlee Posey in his work entitled, <u>History of development of Methodism in the old Southwest,</u> said "It cannot be said the Circuit Rider followed the wagon tracks, in truth he preceded them."

Hamilton, in <u>Men and Manners in America,</u> stated, "Camp meetings and the Circuit Rider exerted a profound influence in extending the Methodist Episcopal Church in the Old Southwest".

The era which the Mt. Zion Methodist Episcopal Church was organized was in primitive Texas, after the patriots had won our independence from Mexican rule, but before the United States had taken us into the Union. The state was known as The Republic of Texas with our own form of government.

The geographic area was extensive. The settlers were coming into the new Republic from the East stopping in already settled communities, or moving further west. These pioneers, in the Mt. Zion area, had chosen to come to what was then the western edge of civilization. There were a few settlers here, prior to 1842, but they were very few and widely scattered. The first group we find working together as a Methodist group was after the Rev. Robert C. Greaves and his wife Saphrona Ann came into the area around 1842. There were settlements to the east, in Titus, Lamar and Red River Counties, but few to the west. Eight years later, in

The Haddock Family _____

1850 there were about 1500 inhabitants in Hunt County and fifty years later, the number had climbed to more than 47,000.

In 1840, a college bred native of York County, Pennsylvania, Rev. Mr. James Graham, and his wife with her mother Mrs. Weathered came to the more populated area of east Texas. Mrs. Weathered contributed much to the spread of Methodism and education in the area. The Rev. James Graham's wife and her mother busied themselves with the education of the youth of the settlers. Rev. Graham helped them occasionally and established some schools in the area, but he concentrated mostly on spreading the Gospel and organizing churches. The Rev. Graham organized the first Methodist Episcopal Church at Pin Hook (now Paris) in 1843. The first church organized in the area, however, was a Cumberland Presbyterian, which began only shortly before. This is proof the preachers were coming with the settlers.

We cannot pinpoint when the Mt. Zion Methodist Episcopal church was organized. But we do know Robert C. Greaves and his wife, Saphrona Ann, were there in 1842, and with them in the neighborhood were Methodists who came in the same wagon train or about the same time. We can't locate Rev. Greaves' Bible which probably has all the record in it. It was kept by the family of the youngest son, Edwin. Edwin reared his family in the home established by Robert C. Greaves and wife Saphrona. Edwin's daughter, Oma Mae, known also as Mrs. Loyd

The Haddock Family _____

Thomas, still lives at Mt. Zion and says the Bible got away from them in some unknown way.

We have always heard of the wonderful Camp Meetings. Those descendants still living at Mt. Zion can recall their grandmothers entertaining them with true stories of those early days, and the great and lasting good brought about even without a church house for their services. But to get Joe Young, who was the grandson of the 1846 Methodist minister James Young, to re-tell the stories of those Camp meetings as were related to him by his mother, who attended them, was a revelation beyond comparison. We learned from him the exact Camp place -others said it was "Over there, somewhere" or "Over in that direction in an oak grove". But Joe Young knew exactly where. The exact spot is down the present dirt road, going north from Mt. Zion church -just a short distance -at a place called "Birchy Bluff." When the Cotton Belt Railroad ran a line through the country in 1884, they made a switch track at Birchy Bluff and called it Dunsmore Switch.

These Camp Meetings continued long after churches built a house for worship and other religious groups were formed. Commerce organized a Methodist worship group in 1878 and steps were taken in 1889 to build a church home of their own.

People from many miles around came to Birchy Bluff for those Camp Meetings, which were a real revival of soul and mental festival, to say nothing of the social fraternization.

The Haddock Family _____

They prepared the all year 'round for those annual meetings. They did this by curing enough meat, making enough lard, drying fruit and lentils, grinding wheat and corn for bread, making kraut and hominy, raising chickens to bring live, and some even brought cows for milk. They brought Dutch ovens for cooking on open fire and added potatoes, corn and meat to roast in hot ashes. This is probably like the present day scouts are taught to survive in the open, except these pioneers prepared ahead of time for the annual festival. They brought along big iron wash pots for heating water for cleansing their utensils and for washing the clothes of their large families. Incidentally, those large pots were used for making huge pots of community stew. Everybody brought along something to go in the stew, which was made several times during the two weeks of encampment. This ultimately became known as "Hopkins County Stew" (see the last page of this section for the recipe).

In short, everything needed for a two weeks supply for each large family was packed in the covered wagon and they headed for the camp grounds at Birchy Bluff for the duration.

The trip alone, without all the provisions, and the year's planning would be longer for most of them, than a trip for us to New Orleans today. Social reasons such as the need to get away for a camping trip, visits with others from 'way off' and seeing old friends met before coming to primitive Texas were not the most looked for treat, however. As Mr.

The Haddock Family _____

W. E. Mangum, an old timer and worshipper at Mt. Zion in an early day, expressed it in an article in the Commerce Journal in May 1910, "They looked forward to the Circuit Rider's, who would come and Administer their theory of salvation and feed the people on Gospel Manna."

Mr. J.A. Rains had come into the area and bought land adjoining the church property in the east. Mr. and Mrs. Rains with their two oldest children, Ella and Minnie, joined the Presbyterian church July 30, 1894. Mr. Rains was voted an Elder, Ella was voted church clerk. Ella later became Mrs. Jim M. Burns and Minnie became the wife of Edgar Ligon Butler, youngest child of James T. and Eveline Cerfrona Mann Butler.

In 1901, negotiations had reached a point of doing something to get the public road designated and yet save their church property. Mr. and Mrs. Rains deeded land on the east, Mr. Charlie Brown deeded land on the south, adjoining the church and cemetery. The Rains deed stipulates "sold for one dollar hand", recorded the first day of June 1904, at 2:50 p.m. Book 50, page 538. The Brown deed was never recorded, but according to Texas law, when a deed is handed to the Trustees of a church, cemetery or school it becomes final at that moment. No registration is necessary. Probably the early State fathers were taking care of these primitive churches, schools and cemeteries, to prevent the expense of registering their gift, and to prevent any future

The Haddock Family _____

litigation with some descendants who may not be as public
spirited as their pioneer ancestors were.

Now, again the church and community leaders were ready
to meet the emergency when in the future the public road
became a reality. This road is now State Highway 11,
indicating that our leaders were able to get it on the agenda
soon after the State Highway Department began to function.
Some of us living remember when it was a muddy road, but so
do we remember when the roads out of Commerce, Cumby,
Greenville, McKinney, and even Dallas couldn't be traveled in
a car after a rain. In 1915, there were cars for the hard
surface streets of the cities, but they could not make the
muddy roads of Texas then. We may say: "Our community
leaders were looking 'way into the future to the development
none of them lived to enjoy."

Our gratitude, and the gratitude of all who pass this
way and see this beautiful cemetery, chapel (or church) and
pavilion, goes not only to Mr. and Mrs. Rains and to Mr. and
Mrs. Brown, but to all others who didn't live adjoining to
the property, but gave all they could. They gave labor,
strength, time and money to make this a beautiful, hallow'd
spot, a permanent monument to all those laborers of the
pioneer past.

SOURCE:

Broadfoot, Jessie Butler (undated), <u>History</u> <u>Highlights</u> <u>of</u> <u>the</u>
<u>Mt.</u> <u>Zion</u> <u>churches</u> <u>and</u> <u>cemetery</u> . Hopkins County,
Texas.

Pipkin Family (from 1st Edition)

BRIEF HISTORY OF THE PIPKIN FAMILY

BY BILLY D. HADDOCK*

Elsie Marie Pipkin was the second child born to Grover Alton Pipkin and Belva May Fleenor. Grover Pipkin worked both as a farmer and carpenter most of his life. He related the following information to me during a visit with him in the nursing home about 5 years before his death.

Moses Phillip Pipkin, Grover's father, was born in Georgia, one of 4 children. Moses' father was in the War Between the States and came to Texas just after the war ended. He owned a river bottom plantation in Georgia and had 14 Negro families at his service. They were freed after the war and he sold the plantation and left for Texas with $30,000. His father settled near Longview, Texas.

Sam and Ace Pipkin were brothers of Moses Pipkin and were both Baptist preachers and lived near Houston.

When Moses' father died he inherited 300 acres near Longview, which he sold for $2.00 per acre. The mosquitoes were too bad in that country and they desired to live elsewhere. They moved near Alba Texas. Please note that Longview, Texas is oil country!

Mary Ammer Lowe was born in Alabama. The Lowe's came to Texas from Alabama four years after the Civil War. Mary's father bought 1,000 acres at Smith's Prairie for $1.00 per acre. Smith's Prairie is located 6 miles south of Commerce.

*As narrated by Grover Alton Pipkin before his death.

The Haddock Family _____

When her father died, she inherited 60 acres of the estate, just south of the old Lowe homeplace (which the Marriotts bought).

It was here on Smith's Prairie that Grover Alton Pipkin was born, one of 10 children (12/29/92). Of the ten children, only five lived to be adults. The Pipkins lived most of their lives in Hopkins County near Ridgeway and Cumby/Miller Grove. Two years they lived near Petty, Texas in Lamar County. Their primary home during the time of child-rearing was at Pea Ridge, located between Ridgeway and Emblem, Texas.

CHILDREN OF GROVER PIPKIN AND BELVA MAY FLEENOR

1. Lynna May
2. **Elsie Marie** - born 4/6/16 in Hopkins County, Texas
3. Ester Lue
4. Leathy Adaline
5. Joy Wanda
6. Bernice Evelyn
7. G.A.
8. Ava Magalene
9. Buford Leon

There is a Jackson Lowe buried at Mt. Zion cemetery in Branom community who is Mary Ammer Lowe Pipkin's uncle who died while visiting from Alabama.

The Haddock Family _____

Lowe is an English name. The story Grandma Lowe told of how the Lowe's got to the United States was about the original relative being kidnapped aboard an English slave ship from England. He was kept on the ship for 2 years before being trusted enough to have any privileges. That was when he escaped. The ship's captain had already told him that if he escaped and the captain ever saw him again he would kill him.

In a battle of the revolutionary war, the old ship captain and Lowe found themselves in battle together. The old ship captain recognized Lowe and hit him with his sword, almost severing the right arm. When this happened, the captain of the colonial force hit the old ship captain with his sword and cut off his head.

The name Pipkin is of Dutch/German descent.

Fleenor Family (from 1st Edition)

A BRIEF HISTORY OF THE FLEENOR FAMILY

DESCENDENTS OF MICHAEL FLEENOR

BY JAMES R. FLEENOR*

ACKNOWLEDGMENTS

I am deeply indebted to Mrs. Anne Davidson Meimann of Jonesville, Virginia. Anne is the granddaughter of Dr. Drury E. Fleenor of Lee County, Virginia. Through her tireless efforts and the desire to learn more about her ancestors, she willingly assisted me in gathering this information.

I am also deeply indebted to many other Fleenors throughout Kentucky, Virginia, Indiana and some other states who were so kind to answer my letters of request. I am also indebted to Mrs. Margaret Davis of Abington, Virginia. Mrs. Davis was very helpful in searching the court records in Washington County to prove the line of ancestors from Drury Fleenor back to his grandfather Michael.

* Additions by Billy D. Haddock

DESCENDENTS OF MICHAEL FLEENOR

The first Fleenors in America apparently came to this country from the Rhineland of Germany during the early or mid 18th century. Many settlers came from that section to settle in Pennsylvania because they had suffered intolerance and persecution in their homeland. In America, they were promised religious freedom. Most of these immigrants settled in the Eastern part of the State of Pennsylvania around Hucks and Lancaster County. Like many of the other early settlers who came to the new "Promised Land", they soon found the areas were getting too crowded. They looked for greener pastures and places to raise crops. This family became part of the Westward movement. Most of the Fleenors seem to have made their way across the Appalachian Mountains settling in the valleys of Southwest Virginia. The best records of this family appear in the court records of Washington County, Virginia. Fleenor is one of the most prominent names in that County today. From this point, this family has traveled in many different directions. Today you can find them in nearly every state in the Union. All appear to be the descendants of the original settlers of Pennsylvania.

The first Fleenors of which we have any record in Southwest Virginia were recorded by Summers. They had settled in that area about 1788. John Fleenor and Michael Fleenor settled in Poor Valley and Casper Fleenor settled in Rich Valley at the head of what is now called Jasper's Creek. Nicholas Fleenor settled at the Lilburn Fleenor place (1903),

The Haddock Family _____

in Rich Valley below Behhams. These four persons named were of German descent and brothers. Washington County, Virginia played an important role in the Revolutionary War. Joel Fleenor and Charles Fleenor formed part of a company of more than 100 patriots under Colonel Campbell of Washington County. Colonel Campbell joined forces with General Green and engaged the British forces in the battle of King's Mountain in October 1780.* Four years earlier, the Battle of Long Island Flats took place. This was the last general battle of the Cherokees for the continued possession of the favorite hunting ground on the Holston. The battle occurred on the 20th of July, 1776, a little over two weeks after the signing of the Declaration of Independence. Seven to fifteen hundred painted warriors gathered at a common rendezvous and entered into arrangements for the bloody expedition. The principal chief of the tribe was Dragging Canoe. There was a fort on each of the routes settled--one on Watagua, a tributary of the South Fork, another in the Fleenor Settlement on the North Fork, another at Eden's Ridge.**

In 1778, a predatory party of Indians came in from the Rockcastle Hills of Kentucky, and made their appearance at the Cabin of Issac Newlan, on the North Fork of the Holston, the place subsequently owned by Michael Fleenor and still in possession of his descendents, some eight miles north of Abington. (1903)**

The Haddock Family _____

* Battle of Tippecanoe, Filson Publication 1900

** Annals of Southwest Virginia, page 1593

In 1756, Michael Fleenor was born in Bucks County, Pennsylvania (Revolutionary War Pension Record--Soldier Certificate 12609). According to his tombstone located some eight miles north of Abingdon in Washington County, Virginia, he was born on November 18, 1760. He listed no parents but did mention a brother, Jacob, on his pension request. From this County in Pennsylvania, he was informed his father removed to Lancaster County, Pennsylvania and to Frederick County, Maryland.

Michael moved and settled in Washington County, Virginia in May 1775 at the age of 18. Here he served his country and state in the military service. Listed below is his service record--according to Chedwato and Supplement Volume 12--Pension Records. Summer 1777: Enlisted as a Private, served 2 months under Lt. William Blackburn, Colonel Evan Shelby guarding the Glede Hollow Fort on the Clinch against the Indians, 3 months under Captain John Shelby and Andrew Colwell. August 1778: 4 months under Captain George Adams and Colonel Bowman. 1779: 3 months under Captain Adam Bledscoe, Colonel Evan Shelby, also Captain Aron Lewis. 1780: 2 months under Captain Edmonson and Lt. Willoughby. One and a half months in the Fall under Colonel William Campbell. According to this record Michael Fleenor served for 15 1/2 months.

The Haddock Family _____

After the War, Michael met and married Sally Lyndar. They were married in Washington County, on December 10, 1781. Michael was 25 Years old. The marriage was performed by Reverend Taylorland. Michael and Sally had 13 children--3 daughters and 10 sons. Michael and Sally apparently provided well for their children. There are many property transactions listed in the Washington County Court House. Michael provided property for their children which he advanced during his life. Michael owned slaves and apparently was very good to them as evidenced in his will. The slaves were a Negro woman named China or Chane and a Negro man named Toby.

On March 26, 1833 Michael applied for a soldier's pension, his soldier's certificate was 12609 under Act of June 7, 1832. The pension was granted and he received $51.66 per annum issued on May 11, 1833. He died on August 3, 1837, at the age of 80. Sally applied for a widow's pension on August 21, 1884 under Act of March 3, 1843 and June 7, 1884. She applied again on November 18, 1848, Act of July 29, 1848 before Abram Mongle, Justice of Peace. She received $51.66 per annum under Certificate 6445, Act of March 3, 1843, issued November 29, 1844. Also approved for like amount under certificate 4605 on March 28, 1859. Sally apparently died sometime in the 1850's. I have no record on this matter.

The Haddock Family _____

Michael made his will on July 6, 1837, just about 6 weeks before his death. He appointed his friend David Campbell and two sons, Hiram and Robert, to be his executors and signed with an X. The will was witnessed by Abram Mongle, JP and Abram Nordyke and recorded on August 28, 1837, fifteen days after his death. Robert and Hiram refused to be Executors, but David Campbell accepted. Bond was set at $10,000, Securities by Jacob Lynch and Robert R. Preston. Inventory and appraisal of estate revealed the following: one tract--1359 acres in Poor Valley and Spur of the Clinch and 180 1/2 acres on the North Fork of Holston River, Slaves "Tob" and "Chane" and Personal Estate; David Campbell-Executor; Appraisers: Thomas McColloch, Abram Linder, Abram Nordyke, and Abram Mongle. Recorded September 25, 1837. A sale of the personal estate of Michael Fleenor was conducted on September 12, 1837. In his will, Michael Fleenor mentioned his two sons, Hiram and Thomas; his wife Sally, and daughter Rachel.

"To my wife Sally, I leave and bequest during her natural life, my Negro woman whose name is China or Chane. My negro man slave Toby desires to live with my son Hiram, and it being my intention that he shall be kindly treated. I will and bequest him to my said son Hiram, and enjoin it upon him to settle the said Toby by him and give him such indulgence as he can with property under the laws of the state." Property to be divided between children --My daughter Rachel

The Haddock Family _____

Price, if living, not to receive anything, but her portion go to her children."

NOTE: It was not confirmed as to why Rachel was not included here.

During his life, Michael Fleenor had advanced to his children an estate worth $15,475. This estate is recorded in Will Book 9-5, dated Feb. 22, 1840. The remainder of the estate totaling $7,7556.59 was divided among the heirs. The total of $23,231.59.

John Fleenor, son of Michael Fleenor and Sally Lyndar Fleenor was born about 1780 in Washington County, Virginia. He lived on the North Fork of the Holston River until his death in 1860. John married Mary Ann or Polly (maybe Ward) and to this union were born 4 children. On Sept. 1, 1819, Michael sold John 86 1/2 acres of land for $1,000. The land was located on both sides of the North Fork of the Holston River. One-half of this land was to be used for the Baptist Church which still stands. It is believed that John is buried beside the church. This is the land which John called the "homeplace".

Drury Fleenor, the first child of John and Mary Fleenor, was born in Washington County, Virginia on Jan. 28, 1813. Here he lived most of his life, being very active in the community. He married Latitia B. Hampton on Oct. 31, 1833 at the age of 20. I have been unable to find any record of Latitia's parents. They were married by David Jesse

The Haddock Family _____

according to Record Book No. 1, page 145, to this union was born 10 children which I shall discuss later.

As a Justice of the Peace, he acknowledged signatures of land purchased by his father in 1856. It is not known at what age in his life that Drury began practicing medicine or if he was trained, but he became well known as a doctor and practiced later in life in Lee County, Virginia.

Drury Fleenor and his wife Latitia resided in Washington County where they had 9 children. About 1858 they moved to Lee County, Virginia with their children. In October of that year their tenth child was born. In Lee County, Drury practiced medicine, often riding his horse late at night to the early hours of the morning visiting with the sick. One story was told of one of his most frightful nights. He was going to visit a patient when his horse became frightened and ran. It was barely in time, as a panther just missed the doctor passing over his shoulder as it leaped from a tree for it's prey.

Generations of Fleenor Family leading to Elsie Marie Pipkin Haddock listed by numbers:

1. **Michael Fleenor**

    1756-1837

    Married Sally Lyndar

    Bucks County, Pa.

The Haddock Family _____

2. **John Fleenor** - One of 13 children

    1780-1860

    Married Mary Ann "Polly" (Ward?)

    Washington County, Virginia

3. **Drury E. Fleenor** - Oldest of 4 children

    1813-1876

    Married Latitia B. Hampton

    Washington County, Virginia

4. **Wesley J. Fleenor** - One of 10 children

    1841-1922

    Married Amanda Redwine

    Washington County, Virginia

5. **John Morgan Fleenor** - Oldest of 10 children

    1865-1918

    Married Mary Jane Mise

CHILDREN OF J. MORGAN FLEENOR AND MARY JANE MISE

1. Effie Lee

2. John Wesley

3. Mary Maxie

4. Grover Cleveland

5. **Belva May** - born in Kentucky

6. Roxie Ann

7. Cora Morgan

8. Maud Emma

9. Bertha Amanda

10. Zelma Dee

The Haddock Family _____

11.   Lottie

12.   Rubie

Mary Jane Mise was born in Tennessee and raised in Virginia. Mary Jane's parents were Lewis and Loucinda Mise. They were of Irish descent.

Morgan Fleenor was raised in Illinois and moved to Kentucky near the Virginia border. He married Mary Jane Mise on May 7, 1885. The ceremony was performed by J.C. Hall. They made their home in Kentucky. While plowing one day, Morgan's team ran away with him and he suffered a broken ankle which never healed properly. He limped the rest of his life.

Unable to farm as a result of the accident, Morgan learned to be a jeweler from his uncle. Morgan later left Kentucky and moved to Floyd, Texas in Hunt County, where his father, Wesley Fleenor had also moved.

Morgan's sister, Martha, also lived in Floyd and married a Turner. Their son was Fred Turner, Hunt County Treasurer for quite a while, and upon his death, his wife Sally Fred Turner, took office and is still holding the office at the time of this writing.

Morgan Fleenor later moved to Ridgeway, Texas where he continued his jewelry business.

6.   **Belva May Fleenor Pipkin**

     8/31/1893-1974

     Married Grover Alton Pipkin on 10/29/11 in Commerce Texas, Hunt County.

End of 1ˢᵗ Edition Appendices

ABOUT THE AUTHOR

Bill Haddock worked as a psychotherapist, business consultant, and author. He specialized in the treatment of addictive behaviors, organizational and group dynamics, stress management and suicide.

He holds a Ph.D. in educational psychology from Texas A&M University. A licensed professional counselor with over 30 years' experience, he worked in the Texas prisons, at a university, and in private practice. He is currently retired and living in College Station, Texas working as a writer and family history researcher.

Made in the USA
Columbia, SC
06 April 2022

58614683R00111